# GOT GOD?

THINGS YOU'VE ALWAYS WANTED TO KNOW
ABOUT GOD BUT MAYBE NEVER THOUGHT TO ASK

ANGELA HUNT

HUNT HAVEN PRESS

Hunt Haven

ISBN-13: 978-1961394285

*To my husband, who for more than forty-five years has poured his heart and life into young people.*

# ONE

## What is the "Word of God?"

Do you have a very good friend? Does he or she sometimes send you an instant message on the computer or a text message on the phone? It's nice to hear from a friend, isn't it? Before computers and cell phones were invented, though, people sent messages to each other in other ways. Sometimes they spoke directly ("Hey, Adam! It's me, God. Why are you hiding?"). Sometimes they spoke through the prophets. (Nathan: "Yes, King David, the Lord sent me to tell you that you're guilty of murdering Uriah and stealing his wife.")

And sometimes God spoke had his prophets write his words down. The written word, you see, lasts a long time. Properly preserved, a hand-written document can last for ages. The apostle Peter wrote, "Above all, you must realize that no prophecy in Scripture ever came from the prophet's own understanding, or from human initiative. No, those prophets were moved by the Holy Spirit, and they spoke from God" (2 Peter 1:20-21).

When we say that the Bible is "inspired," we mean that it

comes from God's Holy Spirit, not from men alone. Therefore it is God's Word to man, and we must respect it. For the next few weeks we'll be looking at the Bible to see how it came to be and how we know it is worthy of our trust.

The Bible is one complete book composed of sixty-six smaller books. Many different men wrote these books over a period of fifteen hundred years, and we can see their different styles in the way they write. But God was the moving force behind all their writing. In fact, the first words intended for the Bible were written by the finger of God! Do you know what they are? No, not the first words *in* the Bible, but the first words *intended for* the Bible. They are the Ten Commandments, literally written by God *to* man. "When the Lord finished speaking with Moses on Mount Sinai, he gave him the two stone tablets inscribed with the terms of the covenant [the two tablets containing the Ten Commandments], written by the finger of God" (Ex. 31:18).

Moses wrote the first five books of the Bible—Genesis, Exodus, Numbers, Leviticus, and Deuteronomy—and these are often called the Pentateuch (pronounced PEN-ta-too-k). Look at Deuteronomy 32:24-25: "When Moses had finished writing this entire body of instruction in a book, he gave this command to the Levites who carried the Ark of the Lord's Covenant..."

Wait a minute—if Moses wasn't even born in Genesis 1:1 ("In the beginning God created the heavens and the earth"), how'd he know what to write? Simple—God told him. Every word came from the Spirit of God. Moses knew what happened before his birth because God told him about the creation, how sin came into the world, and about the worldwide flood. God told Moses everything he needed to know.

The Bible itself tells us how it came to be written:

- Ex. 24:4: "Then Moses *carefully wrote down all* the Lord's instructions..."

- Jeremiah 26:2: "This is what the Lord says: stand in the courtyard in the front of the Temple of the Lord, and make an announcement to the people who have come there to worship from all over Judah. Give them my entire message; *include every word.*"
- Matthew 4:4: "But Jesus told him, "No! The Scriptures say, 'People do not live by bread alone, but by every word that comes from the mouth of God.'"
- Deuteronomy 18:18: "I will raise up a prophet like you from among their fellow Israelites. I will put *my words in his mouth,* and he will tell the people everything I command him."
- Matthew 5:18: "I tell you the truth, until heaven and earth disappear, *not even the smallest detail of God's law* will disappear until its purpose is achieved."
- Joshua 24:26: "Joshua recorded these things in the Book of God's Instructions."

So—does that mean that the men who wrote the Bible were like secretaries? They sat with a parchment before them and wrote the words they heard the Spirit whisper in their ear? Not exactly, because a person who simply writes what he hears is little better than a machine that transcribes sound into the written word. The men who wrote the Bible revealed their personalities and writing styles in their books even as they recorded every word God wanted them to write.

A good way to illustrate might be to think of an orchestra. Let's say we have two excellent trumpet players who are playing the exact same part. The first player might play the part with confidence and an air of showmanship. The second player might play the same notes, but be a little more reserved in his playing. Or his "legato" (it means *smooth*) might be a little smoother than the first player's version of the tune. Or maybe he's feeling sad, and his sadness comes out through the music. Though we can hear their different styles, they are both playing music written by someone else—the composer.

In the same way, the Holy Spirit of God told the Bible writers what to say, and they said it exactly as God meant it to be said . . . while they displayed their gifts, emotions, and personalities.

What is the Bible? It is the Word of God, and "all Scripture is inspired by God and is useful to teach us what is true and to make us realize what is wrong in our lives. It corrects us when we are wrong and teaches us to do what is right" (2 Timothy 3:16).

God's Word is his message to all people—those who lived yesterday, today, and tomorrow. God never changes, and neither does the truth of his word. The Bible is completely trustworthy—and next week, you'll find out why.

MEMORY VERSE: "Open my eyes to see the wonderful truths in your instructions" (Psalm 119:18).

DISCUSSION QUESTIONS

1. Read a couple of passages of Scripture—for instance, Psalm 23 and Ecclesiastes 10:1-4—and talk about the writers' difference voices. David wrote the psalm and Solomon wrote Ecclesiastes, so how do they sound different?

2. In Joshua 1:8 we read, "Study this Book of Instruction continually. Meditate on it day and night so you will be sure to obey everything written in it. Only then will you prosper and succeed in all you do." Joshua was talking about the five books of Moses, the only scriptures in existence at the time. But how does his advice apply to us today?

3. If the Bible is God's word . . . why don't more people read it?

4. Read the story about Satan's temptation of Jesus (Matthew

4:11). What "weapon" did Jesus use against the devil? Since he used the truth and power of the Scriptures to defeat Satan, what does this tell us about the Bible?

5. Look at Hebrews 6:18: "So God has given both his promise and his oath. These two things are unchangeable because it is impossible for God to lie." Since 1.) It is impossible for God to lie and 2.) the Bible is the Word of God, what does this tell us about the truthfulness of the Bible? Can it lie?

We'll discuss this question in greater detail next week.

# TWO

Does the Bible contain mistakes?

What has more power than an atomic bomb, more knowledge than Albert Einstein, and more value than pure gold? The Bible! It is the best-selling book of all time, and its truths have changed the world in large and small ways.

Last week we saw that the Bible claims to be the word of God. Over forty different men who came from all walks of life wrote the sixty-six books of the Bible. But since those men were human and humans aren't perfect, how do we know the Bible is trustworthy? Isn't it possible that somehow, in some way, it contains a few mistakes?

Let's think about it. God cannot lie and he cannot make mistakes. Since the Bible is his word, the Bible cannot contain mistakes. The belief that God's word is perfect, true, and without mistakes *in the original manuscripts* is called **inerrancy**.

The men who wrote the Bible knew God could not lie:

"For you are God, O Sovereign Lord. Your words are truth . . ." (2 Samuel 7:28).

"This truth gives them confidence that they have eternal life, which God—who does not lie—promised them before the world began" (Titus 1:2).

The Bible itself promises that its words are true:

"The Lord's promises are pure, like silver refined in a furnace, purified seven times over" (Psalm 12:6).

"Your eternal word, O Lord, stands firm in heaven" (Ps. 119:89).

Jesus said, "Make them holy by your truth; teach them your word, which is truth" (John 17:17).

The Bible is not an encyclopedia; it does not tell us everything about everything. But in everything it *does* teach, it is trustworthy. Before you start to think of possible exceptions, let's back up and review a few considerations:

Sometimes the writers of the Bible use poetic speech. For instance, I could say, "The Lord is my shepherd" without meaning that I'm an actual sheep, complete with wooly coat and four legs. That's poetic language in which I'm saying that I'm *like* a sheep and the Lord is *like* a shepherd because he guides me and protects me. Just because I'm not a real lamb doesn't mean the Bible is untrue.

Sometimes the Bible writers used round numbers. For instance, in Genesis 15:13 God told Abraham that the children of Israel would be strangers in a foreign land for 400 years. He was using a round number. In Exodus 12:40 we learn that the "people of Israel had lived in Egypt and Canaan for 430 years. In fact, it was on the last day of the 430th year that all the Lord's forces left the land." In this passage, Moses was being very specific, down to the day. In Galatians 3:16-17, Paul confirmed that 430 years stood between the promise given to Abraham and the exodus and law-giving under Moses. So just because a number is rounded off in one passage doesn't mean it's not true in another.

Why do some Bibles use different words than others? Because

the Bible has been translated into many different languages and many different styles. The Old Testament was originally written in Hebrew and Aramaic; the New Testament was written in Greek. Since you read and speak English, you need to read an English Bible. So whether you read the King James Version, the New Living Translation, the Message, the New International Version, or something else, you should realize that you are not reading the Bible as it was originally written.

So how can we be sure the Bible in our hand is worthy of our trust?

People who translate Bibles are usually extremely careful to get it right—they respect the word of God and do not want to make a mistake. However, because people are human, mistakes do sometimes creep in—for instance, in one King James Version the verse "let the children be filled" was printed "let the children be *killed*." (I'll bet they did a quick reprinting when they discovered that mistake!) That's why it's a good idea to consult several different Bibles if you have a question about a particular verse.

Why do people keep printing different versions of the Bible? Different versions are published because language is constantly changing. You know what *the web* is, what it means to *IM* someone, and what it means to be *Googled*, but a few years ago Google and IM meant nothing, and "the web" applied only to spiders! The King James Version of the Bible is lovely and poetic, but it was written in Shakespeare's day . . . modern people don't use words like "verily" and "trow."

Let's say that Elvis Presley once wrote a song on a napkin. Just for fun, let's say he gave the napkin to a man who spoke Spanish, and this man went throughout Mexico singing this song in Spanish. The song became such a hit, in fact, that other people sang it, too— in French and Italian, Japanese and Greek. It would sound different in all those languages, right? But no matter how many times you translated it, you could never change the words Elvis wrote on the napkin. They would always remain perfect and complete, just the way he wrote them. However, occasionally a translator might make a mistake.

Translators of the Bible have made occasional mistakes, too. The good news is that we have many more ancient manuscript copies of the Bible than of any other book in the ancient world. Comparisons of our modern Bibles and those ancient manuscripts have demonstrated that our modern English Bible is very accurate. No original manuscript has ever been found with a mistake in it. Furthermore, the mistakes that have been found in copies are small things that are often corrected in another place in Scripture.

For instance: in your Bible, 2 Chronicles 9:25 says that Solomon had 4,000 horse stalls, but 1 Kings 4:26 *may* say he had 40,000 horse stalls . . . and 12,000 horses. Obviously, which passage do you think is accurate? Most modern Bibles have corrected these small errors either in the text or in footnotes.

Thousands of men and women over the years have given their lives to the study and preservation of the Holy Scriptures. God Himself has watched over His Word, and his people have guarded it, even given their lives for it so that others could read the truth about God and his love for them. The Bible is completely trustworthy. You can stake your life on it.

MEMORY VERSE: "How can a young person stay pure? By obeying your word" (Psalm 119:9).

DISCUSSION QUESTIONS:

1. Before the invention of the printing press, Bibles had to be copied carefully, word for word, by hand. William Tyndale, known as the "father of the English Bible," believed that all people had the right to read the Word of God in their own language. Many leaders

of the church were terrified lest people begin to read the Bible and think for themselves, so they persecuted Tyndale and other translators. In October 1536, Tyndale was tried for heresy and treason in an unfair trial, then strangled and burnt at the stake in the prison yard. His last words were, "Lord, open the king of England's eyes." This prayer was answered three years later when King Henry VIII published the "Great Bible" for all Englishmen to read.

William Tyndale is not the only man to give his life so that you and I could read a Bible—he is one of hundreds who have done so. Knowing this, how do you feel about the Bible you hold in your hands now?

2. What do the following verses mean? "O Lord, you are righteous, and your regulations are fair. Your laws are perfect, and completely trustworthy" (Ps. 119:137-138).

3. Romans 1:19-20 tells us that anyone can know there is a God simply by looking around him: "They know the truth about God because he has made it obvious to them. For ever since the world was created, people have seen the earth and sky. Through everything God made, they can clearly see his invisible qualities—his eternal power and divine nature. So they have no excuse for not knowing God."

Though people can know about God by looking at the creation and realizing that there *had* to be a creator, they can't know about Jesus unless they read the Bible or hear the story of Jesus from someone who's willing to tell them. Creation tells anyone with a willing heart that God created the world and everything in it. The Bible, however, goes a step further—it tells people that sin entered the world and Jesus came to pay the price for mankind's sin. Without the Bible, people would see that God exists . . . and not have any idea how to reach him.

You've heard about people who try all kinds of ways to get to God—through sacrifice, trying to do good deeds, and by observing superstitions. Why is it important that we give them the Bible so they can learn the entire truth?

4. God's word is not only trustworthy, it is complete. Consider the following Scriptures:

"Do not add to or subtract from these commands I am giving you. Just obey the commands of the Lord your God that I am giving you" (Deut. 4:2).

"Every word of God proves true. He is a shield to all who come to him for protection. Do not add to his words, or he may rebuke you and expose you as a liar" (Proverbs 30:5-6).

"And I solemnly declare to everyone who hears the words of prophecy written in this book: If anyone adds anything to what is written here, God will add to that person the plagues described in this book" (Rev. 22:18).

Now . . . in light of the verses above, how should you react to someone who tells you of *another* book of Scripture that is supposedly inspired by God? Are there any other "sacred writings" we should be reading and believing?

Next week we'll find out.

# THREE

How do we know which books should be in the Old Testament?

Occasionally someone will find an old manuscript in some dusty excavation and say that they've found a book that should be included in the Old Testament. Sometimes modern scholars will say that there are books "missing" from the Bible, and God meant to tell us something that wasn't included in the Holy Scriptures. Throughout history, men have risen up and written their own books, then claimed that these books, too, were sent from God and ought to be respected as God's Word.

How do we know that our Bibles are complete? How can we be sure that nothing is missing?

Time to learn a new word: **canon**. No, this isn't the kind of cannon used to fire cannonballs in war. Canon with one "n" means "rule or norm," and when we speak of the canon of the Bible, we are talking about *the list of all the books that belong in the Bible*[1]. These are the books that were inspired by God and written by his prophets.

How do we know if a book has been truly inspired? We look to the people who lived at the time the book was written. Since we weren't alive at the time, we don't know if the writer spoke for God, but the people who heard the prophet knew whether or not he was speaking the truth. If his words came true, if God worked miracles through his name, then the people knew he was a true prophet.

The five books of Moses were accepted immediately, as was the book written by Joshua. Samuel wrote a book and added it to the collection of holy writings, so did Daniel. Jeremiah and the other prophets did the same. And while they were speaking and writing, the people could weigh their words and watch their actions and know whether or not these men truly spoke for God. False prophets were weeded out (Deut. 18:22).[2] True prophets were also recognized by other prophets, who quoted from their writings and confirmed their words.

Judaism, Catholicism, and Protestantism agree about thirty-nine Old Testament books. There are eleven Old Testament books, however, that were written by Jewish writers who lived after the major prophets and before Jesus was born. The Roman Catholic Church accepted these books as part of the canon in 1546, but Jews and Protestants reject them.

These eleven books (actually seven books and four parts of books) are known as the Apocrypha (ah-PAH-crah-fah). If you pick up a Catholic Bible and see names like Tobit, Judith, Maccabees, and Baruch, you're seeing some of the books of the Apocrypha. Why do protestant churches reject these books?

- We reject them because the Jews rejected them. The Jewish people believed that the Holy Spirit did not inspire any prophets to write the words of God after the time of Haggai, Zechariah, and Malachi. Jesus and other New Testament writers often quoted from the Old Testament prophets, but never did they quote any writings from the Apocrypha. Many ancient Jewish writers wrote many books, but no one believes that every writer wrote with the authority of God. And unlike the Old Testament prophets who frequently wrote, "This is what the Lord said," not even the writers of the Apocrypha claimed to write for God. (Look up Jeremiah 17:19 and 18:1 for examples of how the inspired prophets indicated God speaking.)

- The early church did not use the books of the apocrypha. Four hundred years after Christ, Jerome included them in his Latin translation of the Bible, but he said they were not "books of the canon," but simply "books of the church."

- The earliest list of Old Testament books used by the Christian church comes from a bishop called Melito, who wrote about 170 years after Christ. He lists all the Old Testament books in our Bible (except Esther), but he does not list *any* of the books of the Apocrypha. (Whether or not the book of Esther belongs in the Bible was debated for a while before the matter was settled.)

- The books of the Bible frequently declare themselves to be the Word of God, but the Apocrypha does not make any such claim. The Jewish people who wrote the books of the Apocrypha never said they were writing for God or speaking His words. Neither did Jesus or the disciples ever quote from them or refer to them as God's word.

- Finally, we do not accept the Apocrypha because they contain teachings that do not agree with other teachings of the Bible: that one should pray for the dead, for instance. This is taught nowhere else in Scripture. And the Apocrypha also teaches that salvation comes from faith plus good works, but Scripture clearly says that salvation comes through faith alone. ("God saved you by his grace when you believed. And you can't take credit for this; it is a gift from God. Salvation is not a reward for the good things we have done, so none of us can boast about it." Ephesians 2:8-9).

You do not have to worry about having an "incomplete" Bible. The Old Testament books in your Bible have been respected and honored as the true words of God's true prophets since way before you were born. These words have been carefully preserved and handed down from generation to generation so you will have a record of God's work throughout history.

Next week we'll talk about how our "New Testament" came to be.

**Memory verse:** "Yes, I have more insight than my teachers, for I am always thinking of your laws" (Ps. 119:99).

## DISCUSSION QUESTIONS:

1. What would you say to a friend who came up to you with a book and said it was the Word of God? What if he asked how you knew your Bible *was* the Word of God?

2. Science has proven the order of life: the universe was created first, then came the earth, then the land and sea. After that came life in the sea, then land animals, and finally, human beings. Many scientists feel that this progress came about through evolution, but the writer of Genesis, Moses, knew this order and wrote about it long before man invented the idea of evolution. What does this tell us about the reliability of Genesis?

3. How easy would it be for you to learn about God if the Bible didn't exist? Or if it existed as sixty-six separate books? What if you had to go searching through bookshelves if you wanted to read verses from the Psalms *and* verses from Proverbs? Why is it impor-

tant that we know we can trust the books that made it into our Bibles?

4. Read Jeremiah 26:18 and Daniel 9:2. In each of these passages, one prophet is reading the writing of another. Which prophet was Jeremiah reading? Which prophet was Daniel reading? Did they believe the writings of these earlier prophets? Did they act on their belief in these inspired writings?

5. Read Acts 2:22. Sometimes God "endorsed" or "proved" a man's prophetic role by performing miracles or "wonders" through him. Can you name some prophets whose writings were validated in this way?

# FOUR

How do we know which books should be in the New
Testament?

Last week we talked about the books of the Old Testament and
how they came to be collected in our modern Bibles. Now let's take
a look at the New Testament.

You probably know that the New Testament—which begins
with the story of Jesus and ends with a prophetic message—is
composed of four "gospels," a book about what the disciples did
right after Jesus returned to heaven, several letters to brand-new
churches, and John's "revelation" or "vision" of the last days. So
who decided which books belonged in the New Testament?

Let's back up a moment. You may remember that Jesus had
twelve disciples. Judas committed suicide, but was replaced by
Matthias, another eyewitness to Jesus' ministry and resurrection.
After Christ's resurrection, the disciples were called "apostles" and
the apostles were given a special ability to remember everything
they had seen. (Paul, also called Saul, was also an apostle, for he
saw Jesus at the time of his conversion.)

Jesus had promised and predicted this responsibility. "But when the Father sends the Advocate as my representative—that is, the Holy Spirit—he will teach you everything and will remind you of everything I have told you" (John 14:26). Not only would the Spirit remind the disciples of what they had seen, He would teach them new truths and guide them into great understanding. "When the Spirit of truth comes, he will guide you into all truth. He will not speak on his own but will tell you what he has heard. He will tell you about the future. He will bring me glory by telling you whatever he receives from me" (John 16:13-14).

The apostles, who were inspired by the Holy Spirit, wrote most of the books of the New Testament. That's why we know we can trust the books of the New Testament as if God had written them with his own fingertip.

There are some books, however, who were written by other people—namely, Mark, Luke, Acts, and Jude. Mark was a young Jewish man who followed Christ, while Luke (who wrote Luke and Acts) was a Greek physician who also followed Christ. Jude was James's brother. In these cases, members of the early church had to read these writings with an open heart and mind to see if anything in them contradicted what they knew to be true about the gospel of Christ. We also know that Paul, Mark, Jude, Luke, and James knew each other. If Luke had been writing something that was not true, Paul or one of the other apostles would have raised a ruckus.

Last week we learned that the Jewish rabbis believed that the Holy Spirit stopped inspiring prophets around the time the Temple in Jerusalem was destroyed. We learned that they believed that God was not inspiring writings during the time in which the Apocrypha was written.

But then Jesus came . . . the Son of God who was the fulfillment of so many prophecies. Jesus told his disciples, "When I was with you before, I told you that everything written about me in the law of Moses and the prophets and in the Psalms must be fulfilled.

Then he opened their minds to understand the Scriptures. And he said, "Yes, it was written long ago that the Messiah would suffer and die and rise from the dead on the third day. It was also written that this message would be proclaimed in the authority of his name to all the nations, beginning in Jerusalem: 'There is forgiveness of sins for all who repent.' You are witnesses of all these things'" (Luke 24:44-48).

The author of Hebrews says it this way: "Long ago God spoke many times and in many ways to our ancestors through the prophets. And now in these final days, he has spoken to us through his Son" (Heb. 1:1-2).

Jesus sent out his apostles to teach the world and to write the books that would teach generations to come. His Spirit guided those authors so they wrote the words of God for you and me to read. God gave special supernatural powers to the apostles, and they gave them to a few others who followed Jesus. These "powers" were like the supernatural signs demonstrated by many of the Old Testaments prophets. These signs and wonders proved that these people were really speaking for God.

All of the apostles had died by the end of the first century, but we still have their writings. Through the ages, Christians have preserved and protected their books, and we consider them the "New Testament," or the second half of our Bible.

Many people have found old manuscripts and claimed that they, too, belong in the Bible, but these were not written by apostle and were not validated by the early church. They were also not validated by wonders from God. Furthermore, read what God told John to write at the end of his lifetime—and John was the last living apostle: "And I solemnly declare to everyone who hears the words of prophecy written in this book: if anyone adds anything to what is written here, God will add to that person the plagues described in this book. And if anyone removes any of the words from this book of prophecy, God will remove that person's share in the tree of life and in the holy city that are described in this book" (Rev. 22:18-19).

Just as Genesis is the first book in the Bible, for it tells of creation, Revelation is the last book, for it tells of God's re-creation of heaven and earth. We are right to assume that God meant that we are not to add anything to the entire Bible, for He has given it to us as a complete work. It contains all the information we need to understand that God is our creator, that He loves us, and that He wants to forgive us and free us from sin. The Bible tells us of our past, our present, and our future—whether we decide to accept God's gift or reject it.

MEMORY VERSE: "Your eternal word, O Lord, stands firm in heaven. Your faithfulness extends to every generation, as enduring as the earth you created" (Psalm 119:89).

DISCUSSION QUESTIONS:

1. Many of the books of the New Testament are letters written by the apostles (Peter, Paul, John) to churches they had founded or were helping to support. The new Christians had many questions about how to live this new Christian life. In 2 Corinthians 12:12, Paul wrote the Christians at Corinth: "When I was with you, I certainly gave you proof that I am an apostle. For I patiently did many signs and wonders and miracles among you." What sort of signs and miracles did these apostles do? How did this help "prove" that God had empowered them?

2. An ancient writing called the Didache was once found at a library.[1] Some scholars wondered if it should have been included among the books of the New Testament. Let's say you are a Christian archeologist, so you begin to read the manuscript--and let's say

you can read Greek. As you read, you see that the author stipulates the following things:

- Christians must let their money sweat in their hands until they know where their financial gifts are going
- Food offered to idols is forbidden
- Baptism must be done in running water
- Christians must fast on Wednesdays and Fridays, but never on Mondays
- Christmas must pray the Lord's prayer three times a day
- Missionaries are forbidden from remaining in a city more than two days.

After reading the manuscript, would you think this letter should be part of the Bible? Why or why not?

3. If you saw a preacher on television heal a sick man, would you assume that his writing should be part of the New Testament? Why or why not?

4. Jesus told the disciples the Holy Spirit would help them understand the Bible, but we're not apostles. So how are we supposed to understand such an old book?

We'll talk more about it next week.

# FIVE

## How am I supposed to understand the Bible?

Maybe you've tried to read the Bible and put it down because you couldn't understand it. The Bible does contain some odd names, unusual settings, and unfamiliar situations. Yet we are also told that the Bible is God's word to us, and that God meant it to be our "road map" for living.

But how can you use a map you can't understand? Do you have to be some kind of spiritual "expert" to understand God's Word?

No. We'll admit that some portions of Scripture may be confusing, but other sections are easy to understand. The apostle Peter wrote that some of Paul's comments in his letters are "hard to understand, and those who are ignorant and unstable have twisted his letters to mean something quite different, just as they do with other parts of Scripture" (2 Peter 3:15-16). But most of the Bible is simple—so simple, in fact, that parents are to teach the laws of God to their children. "And you must commit yourselves wholeheartedly to these commands that I am giving you today. Repeat them again and again to your children. Talk about them when you are at home and when you are on the road, when you are going to bed and when you are getting up" (Deut. 6:7).

Psalm 19:7-8 says that the Word of God is easy enough for a simple man to understand—and furthermore, it will make a foolish man wise! "The instructions of the Lord are perfect, reviving the soul. The decrees of the Lord are trustworthy, making wise the simple. The commandments of the Lord are right, bringing joy to the heart. The commands of the Lord are clear, giving insight for living."

In another psalm David wrote, "The teaching of your word gives light, so even the simple can understand" (Psalm 119:130).

It is important to understand, though, that people whose hearts are set against God may not want to understand the Bible. Consider the following verses:

1 Corinthians 2:13-14: "When we tell you these things, we do not use words that come from human wisdom. Instead, we speak words given to us by the Spirit, using the Spirit's words to explain spiritual truths. But people who aren't spiritual can't receive these truths from God's Spirit. It all sounds foolish to them and they can't understand it, for only those who are spiritual can understand what the Spirit means."

2 Peter 3:5: "they [scoffers] deliberately forget that God made the heavens by the word of his command, and he brought the earth out from the water and surrounded it with water."

James 1:5-6: "If you need wisdom, ask our generous God, and he will give it to you. He will not rebuke you for asking."

1 Corinthians 1:18-19: "The message of the cross is foolish to those who are headed for destruction! But we who are being saved know it is the very power of God. As the Scriptures say, 'I will destroy the wisdom of the wise and discard the intelligence of the intelligent.'"

Isaiah 29:14: "Because of this, I will once again astound these hypocrites with amazing wonders. The wisdom of the wise will pass away, and the intelligence of the intelligent will disappear."

If God gives us wisdom when we ask, and if the Holy Spirit will help us understand the Scriptures, then why do so many people disagree on what the Scriptures mean? It's important that you understand this—when people disagree on what a portion of the Bible means, the problem doesn't lie in the Bible, but in the people. Clearly, someone is mistaken. Either they don't understand because they haven't been given spiritual knowledge, or they are misinterpreting a passage based on their own knowledge.

Remember this—the religious leaders of Jesus' day had the writings of the prophets, who wrote hundreds of prophecies about Jesus himself. Yet when he stood in front of them, the Lamb of God, born of a virgin in Bethlehem, bound to die upon the cross for their sins, they didn't recognize him. They had the Scriptures, they were staring at living proof of the prophets' words, but the truth didn't sink into their hard hearts.

The Bible is a rich book—some chapters are simple enough to be understood by children; other chapters and verses require a certain amount of wisdom to understand. But most of all, the person who wants to understand God's word must read it with an open heart and a willingness to believe that it is God's word. Those who are not willing to believe will never understand it.

MEMORY VERSE: "You made me; you created me. Now give me the sense to follow your commands" (Psalm 119:73).

DISCUSSION QUESTIONS:

1. Read the following verses written by Isaiah, an Old Testament prophet, and discuss how they were fulfilled during the life of Jesus Christ:

Isaiah 52:13-15: "See, my servant will prosper; he will be highly exalted. But many were amazed when they saw him. His face was so disfigured he seemed hardly human, and from his appearance, one would scarcely know he was a man. And he will startle many nations. Kings will stand speechless in his presence. For they will see what they had not been told; they will understand what they had not heard about."

Isaiah 53:3-11: "He was despised and rejected—a man of sorrows, acquainted with deepest grief. We turned our backs on him and looked the other way. He was despised, and we did not care. Yet it was our weaknesses he carried; it was our sorrows that weighed him down. And we thought his troubles were a punishment from God, a punishment for his own sins! But he was pierced for our rebellion, crushed for our sins. He was beaten so we could be whole. He was whipped so we could be healed. All of us, like sheep, have strayed away. We have left God's paths to follow our own. Yet the Lord laid on him the sins of us all.

"He was oppressed and treated harshly, yet he never said a word. He was led like a lamb to the slaughter. And as a sheep is silent before the shearers, he did not open his mouth. Unjustly condemned, he was led away. No one cared that he died without descendants, that his life was cut short in midstream. But he was struck down for the rebellion of my people. He had done no wrong and had never deceived anyone. But he was buried like a criminal; he was put in a rich man's grave. But it was the Lord's good plan to crush him and cause him grief. Yet when his life is made an offering for sin, he will have many descendants. He will enjoy a long life, and the Lord's good plan will prosper in his hands. When he sees all that is accomplished by his anguish, he will be satisfied. And because of his experience, my righteous servant will make it possible for many to be counted righteous, for he will bear all their sins."

2. As Christians, how can we make sure that we correctly

understand the Word of God when we read it? Yes, we should pray for wisdom, and yes, we should look for good teachers. Anything else?

3. Will the Bible ever contradict itself? If the Bible seems to be telling me to do something in one passage, and *not* to do that same thing in another passage, where does the problem lie—in the Bible or in my understanding of the Bible? How could I solve this problem?

4. Why is the Bible so important? Why do we need to study it? Can we understand God without reading the Bible? We'll talk more about this next week.

# SIX

Can I understand God without the Bible?

Psalm 19 tells us:

---

"The heavens proclaim the glory of God. The skies display his craftsmanship. Day after day they continue to speak; night after night they make him known. They speak without a sound or word; their voice is never heard. Yet their message has gone throughout the earth, and their words to all the world."

---

If even the skies declare that God is our creator, that He is Lord of the heavens and the earth, then why do we need the Bible? If, as we've already discussed, the earth reveals God as the one who made everything, then why is the Bible necessary?

Because without God, men do not realize what the heavens are proclaiming. Paul explains it this way: "They know the truth about

God because he has made it obvious to them. For ever since the world was created, people have seen the earth and sky. Through everything God made, they can clearly see his invisible qualities—his eternal power and divine nature. So they have no excuse for not knowing God.

"Yes, they knew God, but they wouldn't worship him as God or even give him thanks. And they began to think up foolish ideas of what God was like. As a result, their minds became dark and confused. Claiming to be wise, they instead became fools. And instead of worshiping the glorious, ever-living God, they worshiped idols made to look like mere people and birds and animals and reptiles . . . They traded the truth about God for a lie. So they worshiped and served the things God created instead of the Creator himself, who is worthy of eternal praise!" (Romans 1:19-25).

We need the Bible because man's sinful nature has blinded him to the truths revealed all around us in creation. We need the Bible because we needed a Savior to save us from our sin—from our sinful selves. We need the Bible to tell us plainly that we are not God, and that what we think of as human wisdom is usually spiritual foolishness.

Paul wrote to the Christians in Rome about this topic: "Everyone who calls on the name of the Lord will be saved. But how can they call on him to save them unless they believe in him? And how can they believe in him if they have never heard about him? And how can they hear about him unless someone tells them? And how will anyone go and tell them without being sent? That is why the Scriptures say, 'How beautiful are the feet of messengers who bring good news!'" (Romans 10:13-15).

We need the Bible to give us the details of how we can follow Jesus. The Word of God is powerful, and it can speak better than any man.

Many years ago I interviewed a young man named Reynard Valdez. The following is his true story:

---

I am an Apache Indian. Being an Indian has never really been a disadvantage for me; I suppose it has been an advantage at times. But I know my life has been very different from the average American's. I nearly became a medicine man for my people, but one day a ragged Bible came between me and those plans.

I grew up on the Jicarilla Apache Indian Reservation in Dulce, New Mexico. My parents divorced when I was about three or four. My father, an alcoholic, died while I was young.

When I was not away at boarding school, I lived with my grandmother. When I was in junior high, my mother remarried and I moved with her and my new stepfather to Oklahoma where I was the only minority in the entire public school—there were no African-Americans, no Asians, no other Indians, only me. I don't think the kids knew how to take me at first, but they eventually got to know me.

I graduated from high school in 1981 and moved back to the reservation with my people. I tried college for a while, but did poorly. I drifted for two years, drinking and partying. I knew I was going nowhere, like so many others of my people, and I was lost. I didn't know how to find what I was missing in life.

I decided to isolate myself from my friends and search for a way to make life better and more meaningful. I moved into my grandmother's primitive two-room house and sought answers from the Apache tradition.

My people are proud. The Apache tribe was the last tribe to stop fighting the United States in the late 1800's and we still have that fighting enthusiasm. We are proud of our heritage and our culture. The old ways are still alive on the reservation.

My grandfather, my uncle, and two of my aunts are medicine people in the tribe. I thought perhaps the answers I was seeking were to be found in religion, so my aunt agreed to teach me the ways of the medicine man. I wasn't sure I wanted to become a medicine man because I couldn't get used to the idea of drinking animal blood. But I knew of nothing else.

I knew there was a God, in fact, I prayed to Him many times but felt that my prayers went no higher than the ceiling. If there was a way to magically connect with Him, I hadn't found it.

The lore of tribal medicine is not written. It is passed down from one medicine person to another. I spent many nights chanting with my aunts and the others. I participated in the morning rituals. I had a feeling it was witchcraft.

One day my aunt told me that my training would be completed by the spirit voices. I'd hear voices, she told me, and if I obeyed them they would lead me into the things I needed to know.

I was skeptical until I heard them. They spoke Apache.

So I went for a walk outside and prayed to God for help. My grandmother called me to come in and help her fold some clothes and put them away. It was an odd request--Apache men do not handle women's clothes. But she was my grandmother and I wanted to help her, so I went inside.

When I opened a bureau drawer I found inside a ragged Bible. My grandmother did not read or speak English, so I knew it was not hers. I tossed it out onto the bed, intending to use it for kindling to start a fire in the woodstove. The pages were torn and dirty, smeared with chocolate and makeup, the binding was splintered and cracked.

Before burning the Bible, I thought I'd look through it. I knew the Bible was supposed to be about God and I was curious. The voices immediately told me the Bible had nothing to do with the Apache way and not to read it. I ignored them.

I could not understand the Old Testament, so I read portions of the gospels. I read about Jesus casting out demons and healing people. I read how Jesus calmly explained the aspect of new birth to Nicodemus in John chapter three. Despite the annoying voices, I continued to read it.

Several days later as I lay on my bed the voices tormented me so that I held my head and writhed under the pressure. Remembering the miracles of Jesus, I said aloud, "I rebuke you in the name of Jesus," and all was silent. The demons left and have never come back. I knew then that Jesus was real. His name had power.

Before I found that Bible I had never heard of Jesus. No one had ever told me about him. But at that moment I knew that He was real and He was the one who should control my life. He was the key I'd been searching for, the meaning that I had missed. As I lay on my bed that night, I accepted Him as my Savior.

My first prayer was for escape from my way of life. I

prayed for a job in another city and left for Pagosa Springs, Colorado. With no money and no prospects, I stumbled onto a job at a Pizza Hut. The job was mine, but I had to find a place to stay.

I was in the city newspaper office reading the classified ads when the editor walked over and told me about a house in town where people could stay free. I went to visit the owner, a man who ran a Christian bookstore in town. I stayed with him and his family for five months. There I learned more about the power of God.

Later I went back to the reservation. My people noticed immediately how my life had changed. I did not cut off fellowship from them, but I did not participate in the rituals as I once had. There was no church for me on the reservation, at least, none that taught the Bible.

I began to write for the reservation newspaper. In January 1985 my editor sent me out to do a story about a group of people starting a religious movement half a mile outside the reservation. I interviewed them and stayed two hours past my deadline, excited to find people who believed what I believed.

Those people formed a church--really it was just a group of believers in Christ who met in a living room. But I went to a Christian university and graduated in May 1990. I want to go back to the reservation and help my pastor with the church. There are 261 Indian reservations and we would like to start a church on each of them.

I am an Apache. Some of my people call me "apple," red on the outside and white on the inside, but it doesn't matter. I am proud of my heritage and my culture, but I have found Christ. His love transcends language and racial barriers. I am committed to bringing that love to my people.

Reynard Veldez

. . .

MEMORY VERSE: "Your word is a lamp to guide my feet and a light for my path" Psalm 119:105).

DISCUSSION QUESTIONS:
1. On trial for his life, Peter said, "For Jesus is the one referred to in the Scriptures, where it says, 'The stone that you builders rejected has now become the cornerstone.' There is salvation in no one else! God has given no other name under heaven by which we must be saved" (Acts 4:11-12).

Could Reynard Veldez have been saved by being a good Indian? By being a medicine man? Why was it so important that he found that Bible?

2. Many people wonder how people in the Old Testament were saved—after all, they didn't have a complete Bible as we do, and Jesus had not yet come when they lived. The author of Hebrews tells us that just like us, they were saved by faith. Abraham, Noah, Enoch, Sarah—they all believed in the savior that was to come. "All these people died still believing what God had promised them. They did not receive what was promised, but they saw it all from a distance and welcomed it. They agreed that they were foreigners and nomads here on earth" (Hebrews 11:13).

How are we similar to the Old Testament believers? What do we have that they didn't have?

3. The Bible is useful—important—for more than simply telling us about Jesus. It also equips up, teaches us, and guides us through life. Paul wrote: "All Scripture is inspired by God and is useful to teach us what is true and to make us realize what is wrong in our lives. It corrects us when we are wrong and teaches us to do what is

right. God uses it to prepare and equip his people to do every good work" (2 Timothy 3:16-17).

Can you give us an example of a time when you received help, instruction, or guidance from the Bible?

4. The Bible tells us that God exists, but some people either can't—or won't—read the Bible. If someone were to ask you to prove God exists, what would you say?

Think about that until we meet again. Next week we'll talk about some possible answers.

# SEVEN

How can *anyone* know God exists?

We've spent six weeks talking about the Word of God, but how can we accept that the Bible is God's word unless we first accept that God exists? Can we know for sure that God exists, or does belief in God require that we have faith in what cannot be known or proven beyond the shadow of a doubt?

Many well-meaning people will tell you that God is something (or someone) you simply have to take "on faith" because his existence can't be proven. "I know there is a God because I feel him in my heart," they may say. Or "I know there's a God because he changed my life."

Those are wonderful comments, and God can certainly change lives and make his presence felt. But people who don't believe in God aren't going to accept those proofs of God's existence because they're subjective. After all, sincerity of belief doesn't prove anything. I could sincerely believe in the Easter Bunny, but that doesn't mean he's going to hop up to my door and leave me a chocolate egg this year. I could sincerely believe in Buddha or Confucius or reincarnation, but the sincerity of my faith isn't going to make those things true.

Remember this: your faith is only as strong as the thing you believe in.

Have you ever sat in a chair that broke under your weight? You may have had an automatic trust in the chair . . . but it wasn't worthy of your faith.

Two men always cross a frozen lake when they go hunting in January. The ice under their feet is always strong in the middle of winter. Let's suppose they wanted to cross that lake, however, in April, during the spring thaw . . . how strong would their faith in the ice be then?

Be careful what you believe in.

So . . . how do we know God is worthy of our trust? First, as we've already learned, the Bible says God created the world and everything in it. The heavens, the skies, the stars, everything that was created had to have a creator. Science has proven that our universe could not spring into existence by itself. Someone had to create it, and that someone is God.

Not only did the universe have to have a cause, but it had to have an intelligent cause—a super brainiac cause—who created the world in such a way that it was *exactly right* for human life. If the sun had been closer, the earth would be too hot. If the sun had been farther away, the earth would be too cold. If the atmosphere did not have exactly the right blend of oxygen and carbon dioxide, neither humans nor plants would be able to survive.

Look at the incredible, intricate design of a human cell—our bodies are amazing wonders of creation, and doctors are still unable to understand exactly how some of our biological processes work. But God knew how to put all the pieces together in such a way that our bodies grow and develop and fight disease and take in nourishment and learn and communicate. Amazing, isn't it? Could the smartest man alive ever have designed a single human body? No!

God created the universe, our planet, and he placed people on it. Using several different men over several generations, he gave us a book of His words. And from that book mankind has been able to learn things before scientists did.

Before scientists figured out the order of creation, God's word gave it to us: first came the universe, then the earth, then the land and the sea. After this came life in the sea, then land animals, and finally, human beings.[1] Though Bible-believers and scientists often disagree about how long this creation process took, they agree upon the order in which creation occurred—but the Bible gave us the order thousands of years before humans figured it out!

The Bible also tells us that every living thing produces "after its kind"—in other words, a pregnant cat cannot have puppies. One species cannot give birth to another.

The Bible tells us that humans came from the earth—not from other animals, not from air, not from monkeys. Science confirms that the body is made of water and the very same elements found in . . . you guess it, earth.

The Bible tells us that water is involved in a continual cycle. Solomon, who had wisdom given by God, wrote, "Rivers run into the sea, but the sea is never full. Then the water returns again to the rivers and flows out again to the sea" (Ecc. 1:7). Long before scientists figured it out, the Bible described the process of condensation and evaporation.

It's true that some people used to believe the earth was flat, but the Bible has always said the earth is spherical, like a ball. The prophet Isaiah wrote, "God sits above the circle of the earth. The people below seem like grasshoppers to him!" (40:22). Who better than the God who created the earth to give us this view from outer space long before astronauts existed?

As recently as 1840, Vienna, Austria, was a famous medical center. But one doctor, Ignaz Semmelweis, noticed that one out of every six of his female patients died after delivering their babies. Why should perfectly healthy women die after having a child?

He studied the situation and realized that many of his medical students were working with the women right after the students had performed autopsies of dead patients. Dr. Semmelweis instituted a new rule: every doctor and medical student had to wash his hands before examining a living patient.

After that, only one woman out of every eight-four died in the maternity ward. Unfortunately, doctors could not believe that the answer to infection lay in something as simple as the washing of hands. Dr. Semmelweis was fired. Yet in the book of Leviticus, God gave Moses explicit and detailed instructions about how people who come into contact with dead or sick people must wash their hands and their clothes before coming into contact with the living. God, you see, understood something Dr. Semmelweis's co-workers did not: God knew about germs.

We can know that God exists and that the Bible is his word because the Bible is filled with prophecies that either have come true or will come true. The Bible contains over three hundred predictions about Jesus Christ, most of which were written hundreds of years before his birth. *Every one* of those prophecies has come to pass! Human "psychics" and "fortune-tellers" are often, if not usually, wrong, but God cannot lie, so his word is truth.

Finally, we can know God exists because his word has changed people's lives. The people who followed Jesus after his death and resurrection often paid for their faith with their lives—would you die for a cause you doubted? Many of them had seen Jesus, they had watched him work miracles, and they knew he was more than a man. He was who He said He was—the Son of God.

. . .

MEMORY VERSE: "Your throne, O Lord, has stood from time immemorial. You yourself are from the everlasting past" (Psalm 93:3).

DISCUSSION QUESTIONS:

1. Look up the following verses and let's see what the Bible says about some things science has confirmed:

- Leviticus 17:11: "for the life of the body is in its blood." (Can you live without blood?)
- Proverbs 8:29: "I was there when he set the limits of the seas, so they would not spread beyond their boundaries." (Do the seas have limits? Do we have to worry about the icebergs melting and the seas flooding our countries?)
- Deuteronomy 23:12-13: "You must have a designated area outside the camp where you can go to relieve yourself. Each of you must have a spade as part of your equipment. Whenever you relieve yourself, dig a hole with the spade and cover the excrement." In this age of modern plumbing, we don't realize how much healthier we are because we don't have to deal with human waste. But in disaster areas, illness is always one of the first results. Why? Because when people are not sanitary in the way they dispose of human waste, germs multiply and people get sick. Yet God told Moses to teach the Israelites how to avoid this problem six thousand years ago!

2. Compare the two verses. What does the first predict about Jesus? What does the second verse tell us about the prediction and its author?

- Genesis 3:15 and Galatians 4:4
- Isaiah 7:14 Matthew 1:21
- Genesis 49:10 and Luke 3:23, 34
- Micah 5:2 and Matthew 2:1, Luke 2:4-7
- Isaiah 35:5-6 and Matthew 9:35
- Psalm 118:22 and 1 Peter 2:7
- Isaiah 53:7 and Matthew 7:12-19
- Psalm 22:16 and Luke 23:33
- Zechariah 12:10 and John 19:34
- Isaiah 53:9 and Matthew 27:57-60
- Psalm 68:18 and Acts 1:9

Now that we know there are objective ways to know there is a God, how can we ever hope to know him? If he's so powerful and so intelligent and so far above us, how can we puny humans know him? Is it even possible?

We'll talk about that subject next week.

# EIGHT

Can we really know God?

Last week we discussed several ways to know that God exists—we see his handiwork in the sky, we see his fulfilled prophecies in the Bible, and we see evidence of his brilliance and intelligence when we do something as simple as lift our hands and twiddle our fingers. (Could you design the bones, tissues, tendons, blood vessels, and nerves of a human hand? I couldn't.)

Isaiah 55:8 tells us, "My thoughts are nothing like your thoughts," says the Lord. "And my ways are far beyond anything you could imagine. For just as the heavens are higher than the earth, so my ways are higher than your ways and my thoughts higher than your thoughts."

Since God is so awesome and so far above us, can we know him? Yes, we can. We see his desire to know us in the fact that he has given us a wonderful world to live in (Romans 1:19). We see his desire to communicate with us in his word. We see his desire to fellowship with us in the simple fact that he chose to create us.

Jesus told us that he and his Father want to know us:

"No one truly knows the Son except the Father, and no one truly knows the Father except the Son and those to whom the Son chooses to reveal him." Then Jesus said, "Come to me, all of you who are weary and carry heavy burdens, and I will give you rest. Take my yoke upon you. Let me teach you, because I am humble and gentle at heart, and you will find rest for your souls." (Matt. 11:27-29).

When we surrender our lives to Jesus, He draws us close to him and begins to teach us. He speaks to us in three ways: 1) through his word, the Bible 2) through the voices of our parents and the spiritual authorities he has placed in our lives (Hebrews 13:17), and 3) through that still, small voice that sometimes speaks directly to our hearts. When we listen to Him speaking in these three ways, we grow to know many things about Him. We begin to know Him.

We learn that God is love, He is light, he is a friend that sticks closer than a brother. He is like a shepherd, like the bread of life, like the guardian of our soul. He is like a mother bird, like a strong protector, and as close as the shade on our right hands.

Though we can know God, we will never fully understand God, nor will we ever know everything. Some people think that we'll know everything once we get to heaven, but only God is omniscient and all-knowing. We will never be God. We will be better able to use our brains in heaven, and we will learn a great deal more than we ever knew on earth, but we'll never have the understanding of God.

God is infinite—without boundaries or limitation—and we are finite, with boundaries and limitations. Every finite thing has to have a creator, but a finite thing can never create an infinite thing.

Because we have limits and boundaries, God can know us perfectly—our every thought, our every need, our every desire. He can see into every inch of our finite brains and understand every desire in our finite hearts. We, on the other hand, cannot begin to grasp the fullness of his thoughts or feelings because God has no limits. We can know him, we can understand many things about him, but we will never understand everything about him.

Paul wrote to encourage some new Christians to live holy lives. "Then the way you live will always honor and please the Lord, and your lives will produce every kind of good fruit. All the while, you will grow as you learn to know God better and better" (Colossians 1:10).

So even though we cannot know everything about God, we are not to stop trying to know him. We are to study him, to spend time with him, to learn about him by reading his word and walking with him in faith. Then, as time passes, we will "learn to know God better and better." And later, when we are in heaven, we will have an entire eternity to learn to know him more and more. We will never run out of things to learn about him!

Jeremiah the prophet wrote this: "This is what the Lord says: 'Don't let the wise boast in their wisdom, or the powerful boast in their power, or the rich boast in their riches. But those who wish to boast should boast in this alone: that they truly know me and understand that I am the Lord who demonstrates unfailing love and who brings justice and righteousness to the earth, and that I delight in these things'" (Jeremiah 9:23-24).

The greatest thing in the world is to know the infinite One who created you, who loves you, and who has an eternal plan for your life. So many people go through life without a clue as to what life is really all about. They think it's about making money, gaining power, or becoming famous . . . but God says no.

The greatest thing in life is to know God. Jesus said, "And this is the way to have eternal life—to know you, the only true God, and Jesus Christ, the one you sent to earth" (John 17:3).

If you don't know God, you can know him today. All you have to do is ask Him to reveal himself to you . . . and give him your life.

．　．　．

MEMORY VERSE: "And we know that the Son of God has come, and he has given us understanding so that we can know the true God. And now we live in fellowship with the true God because we live in fellowship with his Son, Jesus Christ. He is the only true God, and he is eternal life." (1 John 5:20).

## DISCUSSION QUESTIONS

1. Read Psalm 139: 1-6. How does this passage describe how God knows us . . . and how we can know him?

2. What do the following verses tell us about our ability to know God?

- "Great is the Lord! He is most worthy of praise! No one can measure his greatness." (Psalm 145:3).
- "How great is our Lord! His power is absolute! His understanding is beyond comprehension!" (Psalm 147:5).
- "And we know that the Son of God has come, and he has given us understanding so that we can know the true God. And now we live in fellowship with the true God because we live in fellowship with his Son, Jesus Christ. He is the only true God, and he is eternal life." (1 John 5:20).
- "So now that you know God (or should I say, now that God knows you), why do you want to go back again and become slaves once more to the weak and useless spiritual principles of this world?" (Galatians 4:9).

2. Do you think it's ever possible to *completely* know a person? Even husbands and wives who have been happily married for years don't know everything about one another. If it's so hard to

completely know another person, how could we ever expect to know God?

3. Are you excited by the thought of learning more about God in heaven? What sort of questions would you like to ask him? What mysteries would you like him to explain? What would you like to ask him about your life? About creation? About the world?

# NINE

What does it mean to be created in God's image?

Genesis 1:27 tells us: "So God created human beings in his own image. In the image of God he created them; male and female he created them."

God created many things—the earth, the sea, the sky. He made insects and fish and mammals that live in the sea and dwell on land. He made worms and he made the great apes—many of which sometimes look and act like people.

But only humans were created *in the image of God*. What does it mean to be a creature in God's image? Jesus said, "God is Spirit," (John 4:24), so how can we be in the image of God if he doesn't even have a body?

Let's look at what God the Father said to Jesus and to the Holy Spirit in Genesis 1:26: "Let us make human beings in our image, to be like us. They will reign over the fish in the sea, the birds in the sky, the livestock, all the wild animals on the earth, and the small animals that scurry along the ground."

The other day I heard a radio host say that man was created "in

God's image" because we were like him because we have a mind, will, and emotions. I don't agree, because animals have those same qualities, and so do angels, yet they are not said to be "created in the image of God."

I believe the phrase is best translated with the understanding that we are to be God's standard bearers; we are to be his representatives. You've probably seen movies about the Roman Army and seen them marching and carrying flags with the emperor's image on them. They went forth to rule and conquer in the emperor's name. That's how we are "in God's image." We are his standard bearers, we are and were to rule the earth in God's name, as his stewards.

God is not saying that he will make man to be identical to himself, but that man will *represent* God. He will be God's representative on earth, the "man in charge" of all creation and the animals. Men and women were to rule the creation, including plants and animals. They, in turn, would serve him and live with him in peace.

For another example of this same language, we can look at Genesis 5:3: "When Adam was 130 years old, he became the father of a son who was just like him—in his very image. He named his son Seth."

Do you look like your mother or father? Maybe one of your relatives has said you're the "spitting image" of your mom or dad. Seth must have resembled his father, but were they identical? No. They were very different, but they still had qualities in common. Maybe Seth had his dad's eye color, or maybe he had hair like Adam's.

In the same way, we have some qualities that are like God—we can love, we can show mercy, we can choose to do good. Those are godly qualities, and when we exercise them, we are being like God. But we don't always act like God. When Adam and Eve chose to disobey God, they were no longer perfect as God is perfect. They were no longer sinless. They were no longer holy.

But they were still the people God had chosen to be his representatives.

In Genesis 9:2-3, after the Flood in which God destroyed all mankind except for Noah and his family, God gave Noah a stern warning. First, God said mankind would no longer live in peace with the animals, for "all the animals of the earth, all the birds of the sky, all the small animals that scurry along the ground, and all the fish in the sea will look on you with fear and terror. I have placed them in your power. I have given them to you for food, just as I have given you grain and vegetables."

Mankind was still God's representative over the animals, but now they would fear him. God told Noah something else: "If anyone takes a human life," he said, "that person's life will also be taken by human hands. For God made human beings in his own image" (Gen. 9:6).

Mankind has been stained by sin and we are no longer holy by nature. But we are still created in God's image. We are still the highest beings on the planet. We still have dominion, or power, over plants and animals.

Can we ever hope to get mankind's original goodness back? Yes, we can. Once a person accepts Christ, we begin to become more and more like Jesus, who is God. In Colossians 3:10, Paul wrote: "Put on your new nature, and be renewed as you learn to know your Creator and become like him."

As we get to know Jesus, we will put away our anger, lying, stealing, dirty language, gossip, and bad habits. We will turn our backs on the things that displease God and we will try to do the things that please him. Paul said, "Since God chose you to be the holy people he loves, you must clothe yourselves with tenderhearted mercy, kindness, humility, gentleness, and patience. Make allowance for each other's faults, and forgive anyone who offends you" (Colossians 3:12-13).

The best news is that when Jesus returns to earth, we will be like Jesus in that we will become immune to death and sin. Paul wrote, "Just as we are not like the earthly man [Adam, who sinned], we will someday be like the heavenly man [Jesus, who never sinned]." (1 Corinthians 15:49).

When Jesus returns, whether we are dead or alive, our physical bodies will be transformed into supernatural bodies that will be like Jesus'! We will no longer get sick and we will not die. We will no longer be tempted to sin, so we will be able to live holy lives.

If God is Spirit, how can we live in his image? We can live in the image of his Son. We can smile like Jesus, act like Jesus, think like Jesus, love like Jesus. The Bible tells us that Jesus is "the exact likeness of God" (2 Corinthians 4:4). So when we live like him, we are truly living in the image of God.

MEMORY VERSE: "Put on your new nature, and be renewed as you learn to know your Creator and become like him" (Col. 3:10).

DISCUSSION QUESTIONS

1. Read the following Scriptures. What do they tell us about what it means to be created in the image of God?

- Colossians 1:15: "Christ is the visible image of the invisible God. He existed before anything was created and is supreme over all creation."
- Romans 8:29-30: "For God knew his people in advance, and he chose them to become like his Son, so that his Son would be the firstborn among many brothers and sisters. And having chosen them, he called them to come to him. And having called them, he gave them right standing with himself. And having given them right standing, he gave them his glory."

- 1 John 3:2: "Dear friends, we are already God's children, but he has not yet shown us what we will be like when Christ appears. But we do know that we will be like him, for we will see him as he really us."

2. Are *all* people, or only Christians created in the image of God? If all people—of all races--are created in the image of God, how should we treat other people?

3. Because God is a spirit and does not have a body, the Israelites were forbidden to make idols of any kind (see Exodus 20:4). But God gave us bodies that reflect his character—for instance, God sees, and we have eyes to see. God speaks, and we have mouths to speak. We can taste and touch and smell, and we can enjoy the same beautiful creation that God himself enjoys. When we are mature, our bodies are able to bear children, just as God is able to create human beings who are like himself.

In what other ways do our bodies reflect aspects of God's nature? What else can we do that God does?

4. What are some things you can do this week to reflect God's image? How can you demonstrate his kindness, gentleness, mercy, love, and forgiveness?

Next week we'll talk about something that's *really* hard to explain.

# TEN

God is a trinity—how are we supposed to understand *that*?

A lot of people make a big deal out of the fact that the word "trinity" isn't in the Bible, but you know what? I've written dozens of books, and not once have I ever explained to my readers that I am a woman. Most people figure that out. How? First, my name is a woman's name. Second, if you were to see my picture, you'd guess that I'm a woman. Third, if you were to meet me, you'd *know* that I'm female. I *look* like a woman and *talk* like a woman because I *am* a woman.

The Bible doesn't "spell out" the concept of the Trinity, but it gives us plenty of evidence for the knowledge that God is three-in-one. First, when you read the Bible, you'll notice that God is not alone. Last week you may have noticed that when God created man, he said, "Let *us* make human beings in our image, to be like *us*."

Who was he talking to? Not the angels, because they don't create like God. Not the animals or the plants or trees, because they don't create, either. They are created *things*, not the creator, and only God can make something out of nothing. Created beings can never create like God can.

So who was he talking to? The other members of the Trinity: specifically, Jesus the Son and the Holy Spirit. When we read the Bible, we see that God is three persons, but He is also one God. Deuteronomy 6:4-5 tells us, "Listen, O Israel! The Lord our God, the Lord is one. And you must love the Lord your God with all your heart, all your soul, and all your strength." So God is one—and yet he is three persons.

The idea that God is three-in-one—called the doctrine of the Trinity—is sometimes difficult to understand. Some of the smartest people in the world have trouble with it because they try to apply human understanding to God, who is bigger than human understanding.

Some people say that the Trinity is like an egg—in one egg, you can find a shell, a yolk, and a white part. One egg with three parts. But this is not really an accurate picture of the Trinity, because an egg shell is only *part* of an egg—only 1/3 of an egg, to be precise. Yet each member of the Trinity is fully God, not just "1/3" of God. God the Father contains all of God in himself. Jesus contains all of God in himself. The Holy Spirit possesses all of God in himself.

The yolk of an egg doesn't have the hard shell of an egg, right? But Jesus has all of God's power and mercy. He's not missing any part of God. The white of an egg is missing the egg's protein (found in the yolk), but the Holy Spirit has all of God's knowledge and capability. He's not missing any part of God's essence, either.

Other people say that God is like water: H2O can exist as a liquid, a gas, or as ice—one substance in three different forms. They say that God is sometimes like a Father on a throne, sometimes in the form of Jesus, and sometimes in the form of a Spirit. But that's not right, either, because the Bible clearly teaches us that God is three different persons. They do different things. They talk to each other. They are definitely three different persons in one God.

They have the same power, knowledge, and characteristics. They do differ, however, in their actions, in what they do. Let's see what the Bible says about their differences:

**The creation of the world:** the first chapter of Genesis tells us that God spoke the world into existence: "The God said, 'Let their be light,' and there was light" (Gen. 1:3). But Jesus and the Holy Spirit were active at creation, too. Look at John 1:1-4, where Jesus is called "the Word": "In the beginning the Word already existed. The Word was with God, and the Word was God. He existed in the beginning with God. God created everything through him, and nothing was created except through him. The Word gave life to everything that was created, and his life brought light to everyone."

The Holy Spirit was active at creation, too. Genesis 1:2 tells us that the "Spirit of God was hovering over the surface of the waters."

**The plan of salvation:** all three members of the Trinity were also active in the plan of salvation. John 3:16 tells us, "For God loved the world so much that he gave his one and only Son, so that everyone who believes in him will not perish but have eternal life." God the Father sent the Son, who died for our sins. After Jesus rose from the dead and went back to heaven, the Holy Spirit came. John 14:26 says, "But when the Father sends the Advocate as my representative—that is, the Holy Spirit—he will teach you everything and will remind you of everything I have told you."

God the Father sends the Holy Spirit. The Holy Spirit teaches us, lives in us, and helps us grow as Christians.

God the Father has always been the Father, Jesus has always been the Son, and the Holy Spirit has always been the Spirit. Paul wrote, "Even before he made the world, God loved us and chose us in Christ to be holy and without fault in his eyes. God decided in advance to adopt us into his own family by bringing us to himself through Jesus Christ" (Ephesians 1:4-5).

Even before he made the world, even before Moses wrote

Genesis, God decided to make mankind. He wanted his represen-tatives to have free will and not be robots, so he gave Adam the opportunity to choose Him by giving Adam an opportunity to disobey. God knew Adam would sin, so even before the world began, God knew that Jesus would have to go to earth and sacrifice his holy life for our sins.

Even knowing those things, God created the world anyway. He did so because He loves mankind—He loves you. He wants you to be holy and without fault in his eyes. He wants you to shine in the image of his dear son, Jesus.

God is an amazing being . . . and next week we'll look at one of his amazing character qualities.

MEMORY VERSE: "For God loved the world so much that he gave his one and only Son, so that everyone who believes in him will not perish but have eternal life" (John 3:16).

DISCUSSION QUESTIONS:

1. Look at the following verses. What do these verses tell us about the Trinity?

- Colossians 1:15-18: "Christ is the visible image of the invisible God. He existed before anything was created and is supreme over all creation, for through him God created everything in the heavenly realms and on earth. He made the things we can see and the things we can't see—such as thrones, kingdoms, rulers, and authorities in the unseen world. Everything was created through him and for him. He existed before anything else, and he holds all creation together. Christ is also the head of the church, which is his body."

- Psalm 33:6,9: "The Lord merely spoke, and the heavens were created. He breathed the word, and all the stars were born . . . For when he spoke, the world began! It appeared at his command."
- 1 Corinthians 8:6: "But we know that there is only one God, the Father, who created everything, and we live for him. And there is only one Lord, Jesus Christ, through whom God made everything and through whom we have been given life."
- Hebrews 1:1-2: "Long ago God spoke many times and in many ways to our ancestors through the prophets. And now in these final days, he has spoken to us through his Son. God promised everything to the Son as an inheritance, and through the Son he created the universe."
- Galatians 4:4: "But when the right time came, God sent his Son, born of a woman, subject to the law."
- 1 Peter 1:2: "God the Father knew you and chose you long ago, and his Spirit has made you holy."
- Acts 1:8: "But you will receive power when the Holy Spirit comes upon you. And you will be my witnesses, telling people about me everywhere—in Jerusalem, throughout Judea, in Samaria, and to the ends of the earth."

2. Some people say that Jesus isn't equal to God in power or authority. But look at the first chapter of Hebrews and see what God the Father says to Jesus: "Your throne, O God, endures forever and ever. You rule with a scepter of justice. You love justice and hate evil. Therefore, O God, your God has anointed you, pouring out the oil of joy on you more than on anyone else" (Hebrews 1:8-9).

3. Read the story of Jesus' baptism (Mark 1:9-11): "One day

Jesus came from Nazareth in Galilee, and John baptized him in the Jordan River. As Jesus came up out of the water, he saw the heavens splitting apart and the Holy Spirit descending on him like a dove. And a voice from heaven said, 'You are my dearly loved Son, and you bring me great joy.'"

Point out the parts of the passage that clearly reveal that all three members of the Trinity were present and active when Jesus was baptized.

4. Do you have to understand how the Trinity works in order to understand God? Not really. I don't know exactly how my hot water heater manages to get hot water from the garage into my bathroom, but that doesn't stop me from enjoying a warm shower. The important thing is to realize that when the Bible presents a truth that's hard to understand, you can accept it because God does not lie. In time, as the Holy Spirit teaches and guides you, you will grow in understanding.

This is what you should know about the Trinity:

1. God is three persons.

2. Each person is fully God.

3. There is one God.

That's it. We may not fully understand it yet, but one day we will.

# ELEVEN

Can we ever be "just like God?"

Have you ever been around someone with a cold? You might see someone with a red nose, watery eyes, and a wadded up tissue in his hand. You can tell he's sick just by looking at him. When he comes toward you, what do you want to do? Run! Why? Because you could catch his cold. Colds are contagious. So are measles, mumps, and bad attitudes.

Another word for "contagious" is "communicable." Germs can "communicate" or "transfer" a cold from one person to another.

When people talk about God's character qualities, sometimes they mention his "communicable" qualities and his "incommunicable" qualities. In other words, some of God's qualities can be passed on to us so we can be more like him. But other qualities can't be passed on to us no matter what. Why? Because God will always be God and we will always be created beings and less than God. This "uncontagious" qualities are the things that make God . . . God.

Next week we'll talk about his "contagious" qualities, but this week we're going to look at qualities that belong to God and God alone. Nothing else in all of creation shares these qualities with God.

**God is independent. As an infinite being, he doesn't need anything or anyone to survive.**

We like to think of ourselves as independent people, but even the most independent person needs air to breathe and food to eat. We needed parents to bring us into the world. We need shelter and clothing. When it all comes down to basics, we needed God to bring us to life. We need him in ways we can't even imagine. Even in heaven, we will depend upon God to enjoy the eternal life he gives us.

But God doesn't need anything or anyone. He didn't need anyone to create him, because He has always been—in fact, he created time itself. The Bible says, "He is the God who made the world and everything in it. Since he is the Lord of heaven and earth, he doesn't live in man-made temples, and human hands can't serve his needs—for he has no needs. He himself gives life and breath to everything, and he satisfies every need" (Acts 17:24-25).

Some people think God created humans because he needed us so he wouldn't be lonely. Afraid not. God has always had the other members of the Trinity for company. And he could also talk to the angels. God did not need to create us, but he chose to so that he could delight in us. In Isaiah 43:7, God tells us, "Bring all who claim me as their God, for I have made them for my glory. It was I who created them."

**God is unchanging and unchangeable.** Don't you love family reunions? You walk through the door and your grandma or aunt rushes over and says, "My, how you've grown! I wouldn't have known you!"

Human beings change constantly. We grow quickly, and even after we stop growing, we continue to change. We learn things, so we grow smarter. Sometimes we get our hearts broken, and we grow sadder. We can get sick. We can get tired. We are constantly changing.

God, on the other hand, never changes. The Bible says, "Long ago you laid the foundation of the earth and made the heavens with your hands. They will perish, but you remain forever; they will wear out like old clothing. You will change them like a garment and discard them. But you are always the same; you will live forever" (Psalm 102:25-27).

God himself said, "I am the Lord, and I do not change" (Malachi 3:6).

The good thing about serving a God who does not change is that we know he will always be there and he will always keep his promises. You can trust him.

**God does not freak out.** God has emotions, and the Bible tells us a lot about them. We know God rejoices, he loves, and he feels anger. But God is not driven by his emotions the way people are. He is not happy one minute and sad the next. Because he does not change, his emotions do not veer off in unexpected directions. The concept is easy to grasp if you remember this: *God always loves what he loves, and he always hates what he hates.*

That means he will always hate sin. But he will always love you.

**God is omnipotent.** He is all-powerful. He is able to do everything he is willing to do.

No human or creature is omnipotent. No human can do everything he or she wants to do. I'd like to fly, but I can't. I'd like to be able to swim underwater without oxygen, but I can't do that, either. I depend on God for even the air that I breathe, but God doesn't depend on anyone or anything.

"Omnipotence" doesn't mean that God can do anything at all. For instance, he can't sin. He can't tell a lie. But he can do everything he wants to do.

**God is omnipresent.** He is everywhere all the time. So you never have to worry about being all alone in some strange place—God is always with you. Not just a part of him, but all of him.

Look at Psalm 139:7-12: "I can never escape from your Spirit! I can never get away from your presence! If I go up to heaven, you are there; if I go down to the grave, you are there. If I ride the wings of the morning, if I dwell by the farthest oceans, even there your hand will guide me and your strength will support me. I could ask the darkness to hide me and the light around me to become night—but even in darkness I cannot hide from you."

Finally, **God is omniscient**—he knows all things. Everything, even the secrets buried in your heart. Even the things you think no one else knows.

The smartest man or woman in the world will never be omniscient. The biggest computer in the world will never be omniscient, because it only knows what its programmers feed into it. When we get to heaven, we're going to know a lot more than we do now, but we'll never know everything. We'll never be omniscient. We'll always have the thrill and adventure of learning new things about God, about creation, and about the universe.

MEMORY VERSE: "I am the Lord, and I do not change" (Malachi 3:6).

DISCUSSION QUESTIONS

1. Read the following verses and talk about which godly quality each verse describes: God's independence, unchangeableness, emotional steadiness, omniscience, omnipotence, or omnipresence.

- 1 John 3:20: "Even if we feel guilty, God is greater than our feelings, and he knows everything.

- Psalm 50:9-10: "But I do not need the bulls from your barns or the goats from your pens. For all the animals of the forest are mine, and I own the cattle on a thousand hills."
- Matthew 6:8: "Don't be like them, for your Father knows exactly what you need even before you ask him."
- James 1:17: "Whatever is good and perfect comes down to us from God our Father, who created all the lights in the heavens. He never changes or casts a shifting shadow."
- Revelation 1:8: "I am the Alpha and the Omega—the beginning and the end," says the Lord God. "I am the one who is, who always was, and who is still to come—the Almighty One."
- Psalm 90:2: "Before the mountains were born, before you gave birth to the earth and the world, from beginning to end, you are God."
- Psalm 139:1-2,4: "O Lord, you have examined my heart and know everything about me. You know when I sit down or stand up. You know my thoughts even when I'm far away . . . You know what I am going to say even before I say it, Lord."

2. Think hard—can you think of a single human being who is truly independent? Who doesn't need anything?

Now imagine the most powerful person in the world. How does his (or her!) power compare with God's? Think of your favorite super hero. Are any of them truly all-powerful? (Even Superman has to deal with Kryptonite!)

3. Read Psalm 139:16: "You saw me before I was born. Every day of my life was recorded in your book. Every moment was laid out before a single day had passed."

God has a plan for each of us. Because he is all-powerful, nothing can destroy or mess up his plan for us. How does knowing that God is omniscient (all-knowing), omnipotent (all-powerful), and omnipresent (everywhere-present) help you to trust him more?

Next week we'll talk about character qualities we can "pick up" from God.

# TWELVE

How *can* we be like God?

When we talked about the creation of mankind, we talked about how humans were created in the image of God—in Genesis 1:26, God said, "Let us make human beings in our image, to be like us. They will reign over the fish in the sea, the birds in the sky, the livestock, all the wild animals on the earth, and the small animals that scurry along the ground."

God wants us to be like him, but last week we learned that in some ways we can never be like God. We will never be omniscient, omnipresent, omnipotent, or completely independent. But God has other qualities we can adopt. In fact, there are many ways we can be like God.

Some of God's communicable, or "contagious" qualities—qualities we can share—are knowledge/wisdom, truthfulness, goodness, love, mercy, peace, righteousness. Let's see how we can be like God by examining those qualities.

1. God is knowledge and wisdom. Since God is omniscient, he knows everything (1 John 3:20). While we don't know everything,

we can know some things, and we can ask God for wisdom. What's the difference between wisdom and knowledge?

Knowledge is absorbing a lot of facts and information. Many people go to school and graduate with a lot of information in their heads. Wisdom is knowing how to use information. More importantly, wisdom is seeing the world as God sees it . . . and knowing how to act from an eternal perspective.

A lot of people have a lot of education and yet they are foolish when it comes to matters of eternal importance. "Only fools say in their hearts, 'There is no God.'" (Psalm 53:1). Many people would rather trust in their education than in the God who created them.

Yet you don't have to have a degree to be wise. James says, "If you need wisdom, ask our generous God, and he will give it to you. He will not rebuke you for asking." God will give you wisdom if you ask for it—and if you read and study his Word, you will be well on your way to becoming truly wise!

2. God is truthful. God does not lie. "For you are God, O Sovereign Lord. Your words are truth . . ." (2 Samuel 7:28).

"This truth gives them confidence that they have eternal life, which God—who does not lie—promised them before the world began" (Titus 1:2).

Every time you choose to tell the truth instead of telling a lie, you are displaying a quality of God's.

3. God is good. What is good? Something that is good is something God approves, because God is goodness. When he created the earth, it was very good. Everything good comes from God: "Whatever is good and perfect comes down to us from God our Father, who created all the lights in the heavens" (James 1:17).

Paul wrote, "Therefore, whenever we have the opportunity, we should do good to everyone—especially to those in the family of faith." When we choose to do something good—something of which God would approve—we are exhibiting God's goodness.

4. God is love. Everyone loves this one, and everyone talks

about it. "For God so loved the world . . ." (John 3:16). So when we love others, we are displaying God's love.

John wrote, "Everyone who loves the Father loves his children, too. We know we love God's children if we love God and obey his commandments" (1 John 5:1-2).

5. God is merciful. Mercy means showing goodness or giving help to someone who needs it. In Exodus 34:6, God described himself by saying, "Yahweh! The Lord! The God of compassion and mercy! I am slow to anger and filled with unfailing love and faithfulness."

Jesus said, "God blesses those who are merciful, for they will be shown mercy" (Matt. 5:7).

If you show goodness to the classmate who's being picked on . . . or the elderly neighbor who needs help with her yard work . . . you are being an example of God's mercy.

6. God is peace. Another word for "peace" is "order," or the opposite of confusion. Paul writes that "God is not a God of disorder but of peace . . ." (1 Corinthians 14:33), but "there is no peace for the wicked, says the Lord" (Isaiah 48:22). Peace means a confident rest, a calm understanding that God is in control. We are to do things that bring about order and calm understanding between people. "God blesses those who work for peace," Jesus said, "for they will be called the children of God" (Matt. 5:9). Why? Because they are acting like their Heavenly Father.

7. God is righteousness. We don't often use the word "righteousness" any more, and I know it sounds old fashioned. It's similar to the word "justice" and it means that God always acts in a way that is right according to his holy standard. In other words, he always does the right thing.

God says, "I, the Lord, speak only what is true and declare only what is right" (Isaiah 45:19). When we choose to do what is right according to God's standard, we will be exhibiting God's holy righteousness.

8. God is holy. Holiness sounds like something we can never be because we're human and humans sin, right? Yet we can be holy through Jesus Christ. He died to take our sins away, and God forgives us.

The word "holy" means "sinless." God is holy; he does not sin. We can live holy lives through the power of Jesus Christ. Yes, sometimes Christians sin, but when we do, God is faithful to forgive us when we confess our wrongdoing.

When we lead holy lives—when we do not lie, curse, cheat, complain, gossip, steal, envy, and hate others—people will see that we are reflecting the image of God.

MEMORY VERSE: "Everyone who loves the Father loves his children, too. We know we love God's children if we love God and obey his commandments" (1 John 5:1-2).

DISCUSSION QUESTIONS:

1. Why is it more important to have wisdom than knowledge? You can get knowledge in school—how can you get wisdom?

2. Read each situation below, then tell us which quality of God you would choose to display if you were to step in and help:

- A special needs student at your school has dropped a stack of books on the floor between classes. You stop to help. You are displaying God's . . . what?
- Your teacher asks you why you didn't finish your homework. The real reason: you forgot. You give her the real reason, and you are displaying God's . . . what?
- Two of your best friends are fighting over something. You call them together and help them work it out. You are displaying God's . . . what?

- Some kids at your school are planning to spray paint graffiti on the side of the gym. You say no thanks and try to talk them out of it. You are exhibiting God's . . . what?
- You bring your mom a bunch of flowers. You are displaying God's . . . what?
- Your teacher insists that life on this plant began with a single cell and gradually evolved into mankind. You tell her that God created the heavens and the earth. You are displaying God's . . . what?
- Your best friend belongs to another religion and has never heard about Jesus. You give her the story of the Gospels and invite her to church. You are displaying God's . . . what?

3. The list of God's "contagious" qualities isn't exhaustive—can you think of other qualities God has that we can exhibit in our lives?

# THIRTEEN

How, when, and why did God create the universe?

"In the beginning God created the heavens and the earth." Genesis 1:1.

How did God create the universe? His word gives us the answer: "Then God said . . . 'Let there be light' and there was light.

Then God said, "Let there be . . ." and there was.

The psalmist says, "Let every created thing give praise to the Lord, for he issued his command, and they came into being" (Ps. 148:5).

**How did God created the world and the universe beyond?** He spoke, and it became real. He created all things by the power of his Word. And who is called the Word of God? Jesus. John tells us, "In the beginning the Word already existed. The Word was with God, and the Word was God. He existed in the beginning with God. God created everything through him, and nothing was created except through Him. The Word gave life to everything that was created, and his life brought light to everyone" (John 1:1-4).

In other words, Jesus was with God, and together they created the universe. Nothing exists that did not come from God.

Can we create like God? We can make things with our hands— if you give me fabric and thread, I could make a shirt. Give me a computer and I could create a book. But is my "creation" like God's?

Not really. Because when humans "create" something, we require the raw materials to begin with. You can't build a rocket without engineers and materials. I can't make a shirt with fabric and thread. I can't even create a book without paper, something to write with, and my imagination—and my imagination is a gift from God.

Everything we use to make things comes ultimately from God. He gave us the planet from which we get our raw materials, and he gives us the knowledge, imagination, and tool with which we come up with ideas and concepts for new projects. Even our creativity is really a reflection of God's creativity.

But when God creates, he makes something out of nothing. He says to empty space, "be earth and sea," and suddenly a planet is formed. He says to darkness, "Be light," and light it is.

Even life comes from God. Many people today love debating about when life begins—is it at birth? At conception, when an egg and sperm meet for the first time? No, neither answer is correct. Life is a gift from God—a gift from the word. The Bible says, "The Word gave life to everything that was created," and he gave life to Adam in the Garden of Eden.

The Bible says, "Then the Lord God formed the man from the dust of the ground. He breathed the breath of life into the man's nostrils, and the man became a living person" (Genesis 2:7). When God made Eve, he didn't scoop mud together in the shape of a woman—and he didn't breathe life into her nostrils. Instead, "while the man slept, the Lord God took out one of the man's ribs and closed up the opening. Then the Lord God made a woman from the rib" (Gen. 2:21-22). God took living material from the man and used it to make woman.

In the same way, when a human life is created now, a living egg and a living sperm unite to create another life. This isn't the beginning of life, but a continuation of the gift of life God gave to humans in the Garden of Eden.

We often talk about people who "create" things, but the "creation" humans do is really a weak reflection of God's something-from-nothing power.

**When did God create the universe?** In the beginning. No, not in God's beginning, because he has no beginning. But at man's beginning. At the beginning of recorded time. At the beginning of the universe.

Some people believe that the six "days" described in the first chapter of Genesis are six twenty-four hour days. Other people believe that the six days are six eras, or six ages. The Hebrew word "day" (yom) often means a long period of time. Second Peter 3:8 tells us that "a day is like a thousand years to the Lord, and a thousand years is like a day." And whether or not the time of creation consists of six literal days or six longer periods of time, other Scriptures point to "yom" as longer than twenty-four hours.

Genesis 2:4 says, "These [are] births of the heavens and of the earth in their being prepared, in the **day** of Jehovah God's making earth and heavens—*Young's Literal Translation*). In this verse, the word *day*, or *yom*, covers all of creation. Psalm 95:7–14 and Heb. 4:4–11 refer to the seventh day as continuing from creation to the present. In the second chapter of Genesis, Adam was alone for some time tending the garden before Eve was created. So it is logical to assume that the "day" in Genesis is not a twenty-four hour day, but a period of unspecified length. Perhaps these six days correspond to the six main geological ages that scientists have uncovered.[17]

To further support this theory, consider that the beginning of plant life on the third day required time for the plants to grow to maturity. God could create big plants if he wanted to, but the scripture says: "And the earth bringeth forth tender grass, herb sowing seed after its kind, and tree making fruit (whose seed [is] in itself) after its kind; and God seeth that [it is] good (Gen. 1:12, *Young's Literal Translation*). In other words, God supernaturally created plant life, but these plants referred to on the third day were producing fruit and growing. That takes time.

Another reason to believe that the days are longer than twenty-four hours is the Bible's account of everything that happened on the sixth day. On that day alone, God created the land animals, he created man (who was alone for a while), he brought all the animals to man for naming (a process that would have taken over six hundred hours if Adam spent only two minutes on each of 15,000 living species), Adam searched for a mate for himself and found none, God put Adam to sleep and took out a rib, and Eve was brought to Adam who accepted her as his wife. Whew! That was one busy day!

Whether you believe creation happened on six days or in six ages, the important thing is this: God created the earth and everything in it. He created man from earth, not from a monkey. Man is a special creation from God, not a mistake or the result of some evolutionary process.

**Why did God create the earth and everyone on it?** Revelation 4:11 gives us the answer: "You are worthy, O Lord our god, to receive glory and honor and power. For you created all things, and they exist because you created what you pleased."

God created the earth and all people because he wanted to. Because he wanted to love us and fellowship with us. And he has reasons we may never understand . . . until He explains them to us in heaven.

**Memory Verse:** "You are worthy, O Lord our god, to receive glory and honor and power. For you created all things, and they exist because you created what you pleased" (Rev. 4:11).

**Discussion questions:**

1. Can you create a tangible, touchable thing by speaking it into being? Maybe you could create a misunderstanding . . . but even then you'd be using other people's feelings to achieve your result. You could create a lie . . . but you'd have to begin with the truth before you could twist it. Everything man "creates" springs from something else, but from nothing God can create anything he wishes to create.

2. Do you believe God created the world in six days or six ages? What are your reasons for this belief? (Remember—the Bible isn't clear on this. And the topic isn't worth arguing over. The important thing is to realize that God did create the world in six stages, just as the Bible describes.)

3. Why do you think God created the world? Why do you think God created you?

# FOURTEEN

## What are Miracles?

"Miracle" is one of those words we toss around all the time, usually without realizing what we're saying. "I found this game on sale," we say. "It was a miracle!"

Was it?

If there's a hurricane and your family's house doesn't get wiped out while your neighbor's house does, is that a miracle? If a car is heading toward you and swerves out of the way at the last minute, is that a miracle . . . or the driver waking up?

What is a miracle, anyway?

The official definition: a miracle is God's intervention into the natural world. A miracle is something that only a supernatural God can do. The Bible uses three words along with "miracle" to describe a miraculous event. Sometimes they are called *signs*, sometimes *wonders*, and sometimes a miracle-worker is described as someone with *power*.

When God told Moses to go to Pharaoh and demand that the people of Israel be freed from slavery, Moses said, "Hey—how do I prove to him that I'm speaking for you?" And God said, "I will give you two signs to prove that I've sent you."

In other words, God said, "I'm going to let you do two things that only supernatural power could accomplish." So when Moses went to the king of Egypt, his shepherd's staff turned into a serpent, and his hand suddenly became disfigured with leprosy . . . and then miraculously healed.

Later God told Moses, "I will make Pharaoh's heart stubborn so I can multiply my miraculous signs and wonders in the land of Egypt . . . so the Egyptians will know that I am the Lord."

God had a purpose for those miracles—they would prove that he was the one true God. God told Moses that he would do many more miracles in the land before the Israelites would leave Egypt. By that time, both the Israelites and the Egyptians would be impressed with God's power and authority over the land and sea, life and death.

Many times in the Old Testament, God performed miracles to prove himself to prophets and people. Then came a time of silence that lasted four hundred years—there were no prophets, no one performing miracles. And then—God spoke again. He sent his angel to a girl in a town called Nazareth, and told her that even though she had never been with a man, she would have a baby who would grow up to be the Savior of the world.

A pregnant virgin—that's one of the biggest miracles of all time! But God performed the miracle to show his power . . . and to send Jesus, the savior who would be both fully human and fully God.

When Jesus began his earthly ministry at the age of thirty, he began with a miracle—at a friend's wedding, he turned jars of water into jars of fine wine. He went throughout the country healing the sick, raising the dead, feeding thousands of people with only a handful of bread and fish. Why did he do miracles? To help the people, certainly, but also as a sign—he wanted the people to see that the Messiah had come, that God was demonstrating his power and authority.

Jesus gave his life when he was crucified on a cross. He died there—from the wounds of his crucifixion. Just to be sure he was really dead, soldiers also thrust a spear into his heart. And then— the most important miracle of all time. Jesus rose from the dead. The resurrection was a sign to everyone—Jesus was the Son of God, and he has the power to resurrect all of us from death. If we believe in him, we will live with him in heaven.

A genuine miracle can have three purposes:

1. to glorify God
2. to demonstrate that a person is really speaking for God
3. to provide evidence for belief in God.

**A miracle is a supernatural event that would not— or could not—have happened unless God intervened.**

So . . . is it a miracle that you got an A on your math test? Is it a miracle that your dog came home after being lost for two days? Probably not. But sometimes God works through natural ways to answer our prayers and work his will.

The Lord could have given you strength to study . . . so that's why you got an A. God could have impressed that stranger to grab your dog and remember the "Lost Pet" sign he saw on the telephone pole, so that's how your dog came home. Sometimes when we pray for the sick, God works through the doctors who perform surgery and give medicines that help the patient get better. God often works through his people to carry out his will. He also works through nature.

But sometimes he does something that ignores the laws of nature and logic—he does something only a supernatural God could do.

And that's a miracle.

. . .

MEMORY VERSE: "And God confirmed the message by giving signs and wonders and various miracles and gifts of the Holy Spirit whenever he chose" (Hebrews 2:4).

DISCUSSION QUESTIONS:

1. Read the following verses and see if you can discover the reason for the miracle:

- the turning of the water into wine: John 2:11
- the raising of Lazarus from the dead: John 11:40
- all of Jesus' miracles: Acts 2:22
- Jesus' miracles: Hebrews 2:4
- for whose sake did Jesus perform miracles? John 6:2
- why do we read about Jesus' miracles? John 20:30-31.

2. Have you ever experienced a genuine miracle in your life? What was it? Look at the three purposes for miracles—to glorify God, to demonstrate that a person is really speaking for God, or to provide evidence for belief in God. Did your miracle fulfill any of these purposes?

3. If you haven't experienced a genuine miracle, do you think you ever will? When might that be? (Think about things still to come in the future . . .)

# FIFTEEN

What does prayer Do? Why should we pray?

Prayer is talking to God. Sometimes, however, actual words are not needed, so prayer is *thinking* to God. When we pray, we focus on God and we open our hearts and minds so that we can clearly communicate with him.

Wait a minute—haven't we said that God already knows our thoughts? Doesn't he know our hearts even before we pray? Psalm 139 begins, "O Lord, you have examined my heart and know everything about me. You know when I sit down or stand up. You know my thoughts even when I'm far away . . . You know what I am going to say even before I say it, Lord."

If God knows everything we think and feel, then why do we bother to pray? Because prayer is God's way of helping us focus on him. We pray for *our* benefit, not God's. He doesn't need our prayers to know what we're thinking . . . but sometimes we do. Prayer forces us to gather our thoughts and put our feelings into words, and then to take those thoughts and feelings and give them to God.

**Why do we pray?** We do not pray because God needs to know what we need. In Matthew 6:8, Jesus said, "Your Father knows exactly what you need even before you ask him!" We pray because God wants to fellowship with us, and he is happy when we bring our needs to him.

Let's say you have a puppy that you love a lot. Your puppy needs food, water, toys, and companionship to be a happy dog. You know that he needs these things, and you're happy to provide them because you love your puppy. If your puppy is like most dogs, he shows you his gratitude by greeting you at the door, wagging his tail, smiling at you, and sometimes simply by sitting and your feet and looking at you as if you're the center of his world. A dog uses his eyes, his tail, and his body language to communicate his needs and his love.

What if your puppy stopped doing those things? What if he never met you at the door, never smiled at you, never even looked up when you came into the room. What if he never begged for a treat or wagged his tail when you fed him? What if he behaved as if you had suddenly ceased to exist? If he never "communicated" with you at all?

Unfortunately, this is how many people behave with God. God gives them air to breathe, food to eat, and more blessings than they can count, but they act as if he doesn't exist. They never talk to him, never ask him for anything, and never thank him for the good things he's done. They behave as though they're responsible for the good things in their lives, or they'll chalk their success up to "luck."

Sorry, but luck has nothing to do with anything. God controls the world, and he wants his creations—men, women, children—to look up and communicate with him to the best of their ability. Maybe you're not sure what words to use when you speak to God— that's okay, because just like you understand the wag of your puppy's tail, God understands your heart.

**Pray because you want God to act.** James 4:2 says,

"You want what you don't have, so you scheme and kill to get it. You are jealous of what others have, but you can't get it, so you fight and wage war to take it from them. Yet you don't have what you want because you don't ask God for it. And even when you ask, you don't get it because your motives are all wrong—you want only what will give you pleasure!"

Remember this—God has a plan for your life. Like an author, he has already laid out his plan. The psalmist says, "You saw me before I was born. Every day of my life was recorded in your book. Every moment was laid out before a single day had passed."

Life would be simple if we knew the end of our story, wouldn't it? If we could read God's book and understand his plan, maybe we'd find life easier. If I had known, for instance, that God wanted me to be a writer, maybe I wouldn't have taken all those music lessons.

But—God's plan for me involved those music lessons. I've written books about musicians, and the work was easier because I did take piano and voice lessons. So even the things I now might consider a waste of time have a purpose in God's plan!

When we pray for things that are in God's plan for our life, he often brings them to pass immediately. Sometimes he makes us wait before he answers those prayers. If we have to wait, we can grow in maturity and wisdom before God acts.

When we pray for things that are *not* in God's plan for our life, he says no. There's a country song about a man who runs into an old girlfriend, and when he sees her, he thanks God for "unanswered prayers" . . . because he found another woman who became his wife.

Sometimes we pray for something and God lets us have it . . . along with the pain that something brings. Sometimes we pray for sick people who die . . . and we have to trust that God knows what he is doing even when what he's doing makes no sense to us.

**God uses prayer to change us**. Since God is unchanging,

the person most changed through prayer is US. When we pray, we recognize that God is the creator of the universe, and that he is the boss. If your prayer list looks more like a Christmas list for Santa Claus, you're probably praying with the wrong attitude. Prayer isn't about running down a list of things you *want*—prayer is telling God what you need and then asking him to work his will in your life.

How can you know if you're using the right attitude when you pray? Jesus gave us the answer in Matthew 6. "When you pray," he said, "don't babble on and on as people of other religions do. They think their prayers are answered merely by repeating their words again and again. Don't be like them, for your Father knows exactly what you need even before you ask him! Pray like this:

**Our Father in heaven**[acknowledge that God is your Father through Jesus]

**may your name be kept holy.**[acknowledge that God is the boss.]

**May your Kingdom come soon.** [focus your thoughts on heaven, not earth]

**May your will be done on earth,**[acknowledge that you want God's plan most of all]

**as it is in heaven.**

**Give us today the food we need,**[ask for physical needs]

**And forgive us our sins,**[ask for spiritual needs]

**As we have forgiven those who sin against us.** [remember that you must forgive]

**And don't let us yield to temptation,**[pray for spiritual strength]

**but rescue us from the evil one."** [pray for spiritual protection]

**When should you pray?** Some religions pray five times a day, some three times a day, some once a day. How often should a Christian pray?

All the time! 1 Thess. 5:17 tells us, "Never stop praying." This doesn't mean that we walk around with our heads bowed and eyes closed, but it means that we shouldn't give up! We should always be in a spirit of prayer; always aware that God is listening. And when you start praying for someone, don't give up if God doesn't answer right away. He has a purpose for delay, and you can trust him to always be working for your best.

**What does it mean to "pray in Jesus' name?"** Some people think that to say, "In Jesus' name, Amen" at the end of a prayer is like writing, "Sincerely yours, John" at the end of a letter. When we pray in Jesus' name, we're doing a lot more than being polite. We're claiming a promise that's found in John 14:13: "You can ask for anything in my name, and I will do it, so that the Son can bring glory to the Father."

This does NOT mean that Jesus' name is like a magic charm, and that by reciting "in Jesus' name" you'll magically get what you've prayed for. Instead, it means that you're asking God for something because you belong to Jesus, so you're asking on his authority.

If you were to go to my bank and ask for $100 from my account, they wouldn't give it to you. They'd probably laugh at you. But if you were to give them a check with my name and signature on it, they'd give you the $100. Why? Because you would be demonstrating that you know me, and that I've given you permission to get the money.

In the same way, we can approach the Creator of the universe because we know Jesus and he's given us permission to approach the almighty God. That's why we pray in Jesus' name.

Look at 1 John 5:13-15:

"I have written this to you who believe in the name of the Son of God, so that you may know you have eternal life. And we are confident that he hears us *whenever we ask for anything that pleases him.* And since we know he hears us when we make our requests, we also know that he will give us what we ask for."

When we pray in Jesus' name, we should be praying in the right attitude—in an attitude that pleases him. That means we aren't praying selfishly, or for things to please only ourselves. We are asking for things that please him and are part of God's plan for our lives. If we pray that way and ask for those things, Jesus promises that our prayers will be answered.

MEMORY VERSE: **"**I have written this to you who believe in the name of the Son of God, so that you may know you have eternal life" (1 John 5:13).

DISCUSSION QUESTIONS:
   1. Have you had a particular prayer answered? Tell us about it.
   2. Have you been praying and asking for something that you haven't yet received? Do you think you're praying for something that pleases God? Why do you think God hasn't answered yet?
   3. Does God hear the prayers of people who don't believe in Jesus? Discuss your opinions, then read John 14:6: "I am the way, the truth, and the life. No one can come to the Father except through me." (Obviously, God "hear" everything, but he has promised to answer only those who come to him through Jesus.)
   4. When we are upset and don't even know how to pray, do we have someone who will help us? To discover the answer, read Romans 8:26-27: "And the Holy Spirit helps us in our weakness. For example, we don't know what God wants us to pray for. But the Holy Spirit prays for us with groanings that cannot be expressed in words. And the Father who knows all hearts knows what the Spirit is saying, for the Spirit pleads for us believers in harmony with God's own will."

Next week we'll learn about some other helpers God has sent us!

# SIXTEEN

*What are angels? Do I have a guardian angel?*

True or false: Angels have long, flowing hair and big wings.

True or false: Female angels always sing in the angel choir.

True or false: Children who die at a young age become angels in heaven.

True or false: Every person on earth has a guardian angel.

True or false: Every time a bell rings, an angel gets its wings.

Okay, ready for the answers? All of the above . . . are false. If you answered "true" to any of them, you've been watching (or believing!) too much television!

When angels appear on earth, they usually look like regular people. The only "wings" mentioned in the Bible belong to the cherubim, two of which were depicted on the Ark of the Covenant. Though angels have appeared in bodily form on a few occasions, they are ministering spirits without physical bodies like ours.

There are no female angels mentioned in the Bible, none at all.

Children are humans; angels aren't and never were human.

Children who go to heaven remain human in heaven; they do not become angels.

Does everyone have a guardian angel? The Bible doesn't say so. However, Jesus once warned his followers not to look down on the children: "For I tell you that in heaven their angels are always in the presence of my heavenly Father." We're not exactly sure what he meant by that, but perhaps he meant that some angels are charged with watching over little ones, and these angels always have ready access to God.

How many angels are there? More than we could count. Consider these verses:

- "Surrounded by unnumbered thousands of chariots [of angels], the Lord came from Mount Sinai into his sanctuary" (Psalm 68:17).
- "No, you have come to Mount Zion, to the city of the living God, the heavenly Jerusalem, and to countless thousands of angels in a joyful gathering" (Heb. 12:22).
- "Then I looked again, and I heard the voices of *thousands and millions* of angels around the throne and of the living beings and the elders" (Rev. 5:11). Talk about an angel choir!

**Why were the angels created?** Yes, the angels were created just as humans were created. They have not always existed, though they are eternal. God created the heavens and the angels and the universe, and Jesus Christ reigns over all of them.

**Can angels sin?** Yes—at one point, many of them rebelled against God and chose to follow Lucifer, or Satan. Lucifer was a created being, too, a beautiful angel, but he became proud of his beauty and his intelligence. He chose to rebel instead of obeying God, and as a result he and his angelic followers were cast out of heaven. Most Bible scholars believe that after this point, the angels were "sealed" so they could no longer sin. The ones who followed God will remain faithful to him; the ones who rebelled will be punished with Satan. Second Peter 2:4 tells us that "God did not spare even the angels who sinned. He threw them into hell, in gloomy pits of darkness, where they are being held until the day of judgment."

**Humans who sin are given a chance to repent and accept Christ.** The angels who sinned are not given that chance. Jude tells us that "the angels who did not stay within the limits of authority God gave them but left the place where they belonged . . . God has kept them securely chained in prisons of darkness, waiting for the great day of judgment" (Jude 6). This is just one example of God's great grace and mercy on the human race.

**What do angels do?** Let's begin by looking at what they do NOT do. They do not marry. They do not have children. They do not follow their own plans, but serve God continually. And while the Bible frequently states that man was created in the image of God, it does not say that about angels. What do angels do? Hebrews 1:14 tells us: "Therefore, angels are only servants—spirits sent to care for people who will inherit salvation." Angels serve those who will accept Christ. Since God knows everything, he knows who will accept Jesus. And he sends angels to protect and help those people both before and after they become followers of Christ.

**If humans are created in the image of God . . .** and given a chance to repent, does that mean that humans are more powerful than angels? Not now—angels have great power and great intellect, and Hebrews 2:7 tells us that we were created "only a little lower than the angels." But one day in the future, we will be given the opportunity to judge the angels who sinned. What a responsibility!

·   ·   ·

MEMORY VERSE: "Therefore, angels are only servants—spirits sent to care for people who will inherit salvation." Hebrews 1:14

DISCUSSION QUESTIONS:

1. Since angels are sent to minister to humans, read the following verses and explain how the angel served the man or woman involved:

- Matthew 4:10-12
- Genesis 16:7
- Genesis 19:15
- Exodus 23:20
- Matthew 1:20
- Matthew 28:5
- Luke 1:13
- Luke 22:43
- Acts 5:19

2. There are many types of angels and differing ranks of angels. And while one of their jobs is to serve God's children, they also obey him in other things. Hebrews 13:2 says, "Don't forget to show hospitality to strangers, for some who have done this have entertained angels without realizing it!" Do you know anyone who claims to have seen an angel?

Next week we'll talk about angels who rebelled against God.

## 17 WHO IS THE DEVIL? WHAT ARE DEMONS?

WHEN GOD first created the world, everything was good—perfect, in fact. But soon after Adam and Eve began to live in the Garden, we see Satan, in the form of a serpent, deciding to tempt Eve and entice her away from God. So at some point between God's original creation of the universe—including the angelic kingdoms—Satan led a heavenly revolt and many of the angels went disobeyed God along with him.

Satan, also known as Lucifer, was once a beautiful angel with great authority. The prophet Isaiah referred to Lucifer when he wrote, "How you are fallen from heaven, O shining star, son of the morning! You have been thrown down to the earth, you who destroyed the nations of the world. For you said to yourself, 'I will ascend to heaven and set my throne above God's stars. I will preside on the mountain of the gods far away in the north. I will climb to the highest heavens and be like the Most High. Instead, you will be brought down to the place of the dead, down to its lowest depths."

Like man, angels were created with the freedom to choose to obey or disobey God. Lucifer is an angel, nothing more, who chose to disobey his creator. Many of the angels followed him in disobedience, and, like him, they will suffer for their sin.

Why did God create these angels, knowing that they would rebel? I can't read God's mind, but I trust his plan. And even these angels serve a purpose in eternity.

What if I offered you a choice between two ice cream cones that were both the same size and both filled with vanilla ice cream. A choice between vanilla and vanilla isn't much of a choice, is it? If we did not have the freedom to choose good from evil, we would not have free choice. We would love God because we had no other option, and he wants us to love him because we choose to love him.

What are demons? Should we be afraid of them? Demons are angels who sinned against God and now work evil in the world. They serve Satan, not God. The Bible tells us that demons "did not stay within the limits of authority God gave them but left the place where they belonged . . . God has kept them securely chained in prisons of darkness, waiting for the great day of judgment" (Jude 6).

In 2 Peter 2:4 we read: "God did not spare even the angels who sinned. He threw them into hell, in gloomy pits of darkness, where they are being held until the day of judgment."

Does that mean that fallen angels are in hell now? Not the *hell* you think of when you think of a lake of fire. These fallen angels have been thrown into darkness, which is another way of saying that they have been prohibited access to heaven. They are condemned to wander on the earth and in dark places apart from the glory of God. Of course, they cannot escape God's presence, for he is everywhere, but they are chained and cannot return to their former places in heaven. While they are awaiting judgment—which will come later—they can and do work evil in the world.

Does everything bad in the world come from demons? No. If you are tired or sick, you may simply be tired and sick—it's not likely that a demon is making you tired and sick. If a friend is addicted to cigarettes, it's not likely that a demon is making him addicted. If two Christians are arguing, it's not likely that a demon is making them argue—it may be their pride that is getting in the way of agreement. Even Christians sin, so we have to watch out for pride and selfishness and habits that are not good for us.

Should I be afraid of the devil or demons? No. A lot of Christians quote 1 Peter 5:8 when they speak of the devil: "Stay alert! Watch out for your great enemy, the devil. He prowls around like a roaring lion, looking for someone to devour."

Peter's warning should not be taken as proof that the devil can eat you alive! No way! Because even the devil and the demons are under God's control, now and forever. If you read the story of Job, you'll realize that Satan could not touch Job without God's permission. Jesus could cast out demons with a word. Demons are harnessed by "eternal chains" and they are not stronger than Jesus.

Neither is Satan. He may roam about like a lion, but always remember this: that lion is on a leash, and the other end of the leash is firmly in God's hand!

So what do demons do? They fool people. You may have seen movies where demons do all kinds of scary things, but that's what Hollywood thinks of demons. Demons can do scary things, but they're much more likely to do beautiful things in order to fool people into following false religions. Because Satan hates God, he wants to keep people from following God. So he uses every trick in his book, not to convince people to follow him, but to follow *anything but God.*

Demons are active in many false religions today. People who follow eastern religions often talk of their "spirit guides" to help them "discover the god within." Don't be fooled. These are demons and they're using the same line Satan used on Eve: "You can be like God."

Demons are real, and the best way to protect yourself against their evil is to remain strong in Christ. John wrote, "But you belong to God, my dear children. You have already won a victory over those people, because the Spirit who lives in you is greater than the spirit who lives in the world" (1 John 4:4).

The devil is not God. He is not omniscient; he doesn't know everything. He's not everywhere. He can't read your thoughts. He's not all-powerful. And he's on that leash.

The Spirit of God, which lives inside every true believer in Christ, is greater than the devil or any demon. You do not need to fear them, but you should also be careful not to fool around with things like Oujia boards, séances, and horoscopes. If you look to a board or a ghost or the stars for influence over your life, you are *not* looking to God or fully trusting him. The Bible strongly tells us to avoid such things, because many an innocent young person has opened the door to the influence of demons by talking to "spirits" he "met" during a board game or séance.

Guard your heart. Entrust it to God alone. And know that no fallen angel is stronger than Jesus.

MEMORY VERSE: "But you belong to God, my dear children. You have already won a victory over those people, because the Spirit who lives in you is greater than the spirit who lives in the world" (1 John 4:4).

DISCUSSION QUESTIONS:

1. After reading this lesson, did you learn anything new about demons or the devil?

2. Do you know anyone who relies on a horoscope or fortune teller? Do your friends play with a Ouija board? What will you say to them the next time this subject comes up?

3. When the devil came to tempt Jesus, Jesus did something specific to resist the devil. What did he do? If you need help, read the story in Matthew 4:1-11.

# SEVENTEEN

Where's heaven? And how long will we be there?

*Heaven.* When we hear the word, most of us imagine people in white robes, sitting on clouds and strumming harps. In fact, if we were honest, we have to admit that an eternity of cloud-sitting and harp-strumming sounds downright boring!

If you think that's all heaven is, you're sadly mistaken. Heaven is God's home, and right now it probably exists in a dimension we can't even see.

I read an interesting book the other day called *Flatland,* by Edwin Abbott. The book is about a group of beings that live in only two dimensions. Imagine, if you can, a tabletop covered with construction paper circles and squares and rectangles and lines. Now imagine that you ARE one of those paper circles or squares or rectangles or lines. If you lived in a flat world and could see only north, south, east, and west, but not *above* or *beneath,* you'd be living in Flatland. If you lived in Flatland and saw a circle approaching, it wouldn't look like a circle—it'd look like a straight line. So would a rectangle. And a straight line, coming toward you, would look like a dot.

Because you could not rise above the table and look down on Flatland, you'd never have any idea that things looked different from another dimension. You wouldn't even know there was another dimension, unless a three-dimensional person appeared in your world and tried to explain that *there is more to imagine.*

We humans get so used to living in our world that we forget that there is much more to imagine and to believe. God created this world with height and breadth and width, but other dimensions exist. We have eternal souls that cannot be seen or measured. We are surrounded by angels—good and evil—that we cannot see unless God reveals them to us. God sits on a throne in heaven, which is located in a dimension we cannot access—yet.

But one day we will enter heaven with supernatural bodies equipped for life in a new dimension. We will also be able to enjoy a new earth, a planet recreated and repopulated with animals and plants and mountains. We will be part of God's family, with thousands of new brothers and sisters who love us. We will be able to do all the things we enjoyed doing in this life, but we won't be badgered by sin or temptation. The sinful part of our nature will be gone, and we will be joyful and content to live in God's presence for eternity.

When you arrive in heaven, you will feel as though you have finally come home—and it will be a place so much greater than anything you could ever have imagined. This earth will feel like Flatland compared to the rich diversity of heaven. Best of all, you will live there for eternity.

How long is eternity? Forever and ever. Longer than you can imagine.

. . .

MEMORY VERSE: "No eye has seen, no ear has heard, and no mind has imagined what God has prepared for those who love him" (1 Cor. 2:9).


DISCUSSION QUESTIONS:

Read the following verses and explain what they tell us about heaven:

John 14:1-2: "Don't let your hearts be troubled. Trust in God, and trust also in me. There is more than enough room in my Father's home. If this were not so, would I have told you that I am going to prepare a place for you?"

"No eye has seen, no ear has heard, and no mind has imagined what God has prepared for those who love him. But it was to us that God revealed these things by his Spirit." (1 Cor. 2:9-10).

"Marriage is for people here on earth. But in the age to come, those worthy of being raised from the dead will neither marry nor be given in marriage. And they will never die again. In this respect they will be like angels. They are children of God and children of the resurrection." (Luke 20:34-36)

"All these people died still believing what God has promised them. They did not receive what was promised, but they all saw it from a distance and welcomed it. They agreed that they were foreigners and nomads here on earth. . . . But they were looking for a better place, a heavenly homeland. That is why God is not ashamed to be called their God, for he has prepared a city for them" (Hebrews 11:13, 16).

"Then I saw a new heaven and a new earth, for the old heaven and the old earth had disappeared. And the sea was also gone. And I saw the holy city, the new Jerusalem, coming down from God out of heaven . . ." (Rev. 21:1-2, description includes entire chapter).

2. What do you think heaven will be like? How has this lesson changed your view of heaven?

Even if you don't understand it all, know this: God has prepared a place for his children, and it will be a wonderful, glorious place. You can trust him.

# NOTES

## Chapter 3

1. Wayne Grudem, *Systematic Theology*, p. 54.
2. Norman Geisler, *Systematic Theology*, Volume 1, p. 523.

## Chapter 4

1. Wayne Grudem, p. 67.

## Chapter 7

1. Dr. Norman Geisler, *Systematic Theology: Volume One*, p. 545.

## Chapter 13

1. [7] Gleason L. Archer, *A Survey of Old Testament Introduction* (Chicago: Moody Press, 1994), 196–203.

# ABOUT THE AUTHOR

With over five million copies of her books sold worldwide, Angela Hunt is the best-selling author of more than 160 works ranging from picture books (*The Tale of Three Trees*) to novels and nonfiction.

Now that her two children are grown, Angie and her husband live in Florida with Very Big Dogs (a direct result of watching *Turner and Hooch* too many times). This love for mastiffs has not been without its rewards—one of their dogs was featured on *Live with Regis and Kelly* as the second-largest canine in America. Their dog received this unique honor after an all-expenses-paid trip to Manhattan for the dog and the Hunts, complete with VIP air travel and a stretch limo in which they toured New York City. Afterward, the dog gave out pawtographs at the airport.

Angela admits to being fascinated by animals, medicine, unexplained phenomena, and "just about everything."

Her books have won the coveted Christy Award, several Angel Awards from Excellence in Media, and the Gold and Silver Medallions from *Foreword Magazine*'s Book of the Year Award. In 2007, her novel *The Note* was featured as a Christmas movie on the Hallmark channel. She recently completed her doctorate in biblical literature and is now finishing her doctorate in Theology.

When she's not home writing, Angie often travels to teach writing workshops at schools and writers' conferences. And to talk about her dogs, of course. Readers may visit her web site at **www.ange lahuntbooks.com**.